Common Sense Questions about Learners

Other Books by the Author

Solving Education's Problems Effectively: A Guide to Using the Case Method

Cockeyed Education: A Case Method Primer

Lopsided Schools: Case Method Briefings

Capping Costs: Putting a Price Tag on School Reform

Teachers Go to Rehab: Historical and Current Advice to Instructors

Common Sense Questions about Instruction: The Answers Can Provide Essential Steps to Improvement

Common Sense Questions about School Administration: The Answers Can Provide Essential Steps to Improvement

Common Sense Questions about Tests: The Answers Can Reveal Essential Steps for Improvement

Common Sense Questions about Learners: The Answers Can Reveal Essential Steps for Improvement

Common Sense Questions about Learners

The Answers Can Reveal Essential Steps for Improvement

Gerard Giordano

ROWMAN & LITTLEFIELD
Lanham • Boulder • New York • London

Published by Rowman & Littlefield
A wholly owned subsidiary of The Rowman & Littlefield Publishing Group, Inc.
4501 Forbes Boulevard, Suite 200, Lanham, Maryland 20706
www.rowman.com

Unit A, Whitacre Mews, 26–34 Stannary Street, London SE11 4AB

Copyright © 2017 by Gerard Giordano

All rights reserved. No part of this book may be reproduced in any form or by any electronic or mechanical means, including information storage and retrieval systems, without written permission from the publisher, except by a reviewer who may quote passages in a review.

British Library Cataloguing in Publication Information Available

Library of Congress Cataloging-in-Publication Data Available

ISBN 978-1-4758-3013-2 (cloth : alk. paper)
ISBN 978-1-4758-3014-9 (pbk. : alk. paper)
ISBN 978-1-4758-3015-6 (electronic)

∞™ The paper used in this publication meets the minimum requirements of American National Standard for Information Sciences—Permanence of Paper for Printed Library Materials, ANSI/NISO Z39.48–1992.

Printed in the United States of America

The highlights of my days are my classroom dialogues with students.
This book, which summarizes those dialogues, is dedicated to them.

Contents

List of Tables	ix
Preface	xiii
Acknowledgment	xix
1 Who Should Take Charge of Educational Funding?	1
2 Who Should Take Charge of School Menus?	13
3 Who Should Take Charge of Students' Smartphones?	25
4 Who Should Take Charge of Assessment?	37
5 Who Should Take Charge of Grading?	47
6 Who Should Take Charge of Truants?	57
7 Who Should Take Charge of Training Principals?	67
8 Who Should Take Charge of School Technology?	77
9 Who Should Take Charge of Privatizing Public Schools?	87
10 Who Should Take Charge of Tests?	97
References	107
About the Author	123

List of Tables

1.1.	Presidents Recommend That Their College Continue Operating	9
1.2.	An Interim President Recommends That His College Cease Operating	9
1.3.	New York's Governors Recommend Modest Public Funds for Private Schools	10
1.4.	A New York Governor Recommends Substantial Public Funds for Private Schools	11
2.1.	Restaurant Executives Provide Colossal-Sized Portions and Endless Breadsticks	20
2.2.	Restaurant Executives Downsize Portions and Limit Breadsticks	21
2.3.	Restaurant Executives Reconfigure Leasing Arrangements	21
2.4.	School Cafeteria Managers Provide Large Portions of Not-Always-Healthy Foods	22
2.5.	School Cafeteria Managers Provide Small Portions of Healthy Foods	22
2.6.	School Cafeteria Managers Campaign against Federal Lunch Regulations	23
3.1.	T-Mobile Executives Take Marketers' Advice about Smartphone Plans	33
3.2.	T-Mobile Executives Ignore Marketers' Advice about Smartphone Plans	33
3.3.	New York City's Mayor Takes Educators' Advice about Students' Smartphones	34
3.4.	New York City's Mayor Ignores Educators' Advice about Students' Smartphones	35

4.1.	Fiscal Analysts Ignore Indirect Benefits of Governmental Initiatives	43
4.2.	Fiscal Analysts Highlight Indirect Benefits of Governmental Initiatives	43
4.3.	Scholastic Analysts Ignore Extraneous Influences on Test Scores	44
4.4.	Scholastic Analysts Highlight Extraneous Influences on Test Scores	45
5.1.	Attorneys Rely on Technical Experts to Design Courtroom Videos	53
5.2.	Attorneys Personally Design Courtroom Videos	53
5.3.	Politicians Rely on School Administrators to Develop Grading Policies	54
5.4.	Politicians Personally Develop Grading Policies	55
6.1.	A New York City Mayor Endorses a Local Plan for Pedestrian-Friendly Plazas	63
6.2.	A New York City Mayor Devises His Own Plan for Pedestrian-Friendly Plazas	64
6.3.	Legislators Endorse Local Plans for Truant Students	64
6.4.	Legislators Devise Their Own Plans for Truant Students	65
7.1.	Businesspeople Provide Alternative Training for Artists	74
7.2.	Businesspeople Defend Their Alternative Training for Artists	74
7.3.	Businesspeople Provide Alternative Training for Chicago's Principals	75
7.4.	Businesspeople Defend Their Alternative Training for Chicago's Principals	76
8.1.	Law School Administrators Highlight Graduates with Permanent Jobs	84
8.2.	Law School Administrators Highlight Graduates with Temporary Jobs	85
8.3.	Public School Administrators Highlight Students' Test Scores	85
8.4.	Public School Administrators Highlight Students' Access to iPads	86
9.1.	School Administrators Delegate Disciplinary Authority to Teachers	93
9.2.	School Administrators Limit the Disciplinary Authority of Teachers	94
9.3.	California Legislators Give Schoolboards Authority for Privatizing Public Schools	95

9.4.	California Legislators Limit Schoolboards' Authority for Privatizing Public Schools	95
10.1.	Marketers Use Phone Ads Infrequently	103
10.2.	Marketers Use Phone Ads Frequently	104
10.3.	New York's Regents Administer Tests Infrequently	104
10.4.	New York's Regents Administer Tests Frequently	105

Preface

Who Should Take Charge of Learners?

> [Dog whistles] mean one thing to the general population but have a different meaning for a targeted . . . audience.
> —Taegan Goddard, 2015

> [My political adversary has been using] dog whistle terms.
> —Former Florida Governor Jeb Bush, quoted by Stokols, 2015

> [My political adversary has been] dog whistling for an entire year.
> —Former Vermont Governor Howard Dean, quoted by Key, 2016

> [They] accused [their political adversary] of dog-whistling.
> —Emily Badger, 2016

Novice political candidates worried that they might not get enough votes to win offices. Veterans worried that they might not get enough votes to stay in them.

Candidates realized that one of the best ways to secure votes was to run effective campaigns. However, they frequently needed significant funds.

The candidates turned to their parties for some of the funding that they needed. They turned to rich individuals, well-financed groups, affluent organizations, and successful corporations for the rest.

When George W. Bush was running for president, he asked businesspeople to help pay for his campaign. He promised that he would help them in return. He explained that he would accelerate economic growth, relax financial regulations, provide more military contracts, and aid learners in the nations' schools.

Most businesspeople were excited by Bush's plans to spur economic growth, relax financial regulations, and increase military spending. They detected obvious benefits for their firms.

Only some of the businesspeople detected any benefits for the plan to help learners. Those who were most excited had an ulterior motive: they wished to protect the investments that they had made in for-profit schooling and commercial testing.

Bush was not at all disconcerted by the quid-pro-quo proposal from businesspeople. He had agreed to proposals of this sort during his gubernatorial campaign in Texas. He was pleased when they attracted hardly any criticism.

Bush was ready to collaborate with the businesspeople again. Nonetheless, he was nervous about the scrutiny that he would draw during a presidential campaign.

* * * * *

Bush needed a subtle way to send signals to business donors. He eventually came up with the ideal technique. He patterned it after one that animal trainers use with dogs (Dictionary.com, 2015; Krugman, 2014; McCutcheon, 2014; Zimmer, 2014).

Animal trainers blow into whistles that seem to create no sound. However, the whistles actually produce high-pitched tones that only dogs can detect.

Bush was under pressure to establish policies that would protect his donors' educational investments. When he was ready to share information about those policies, he used a dog whistle: he embedded the information within a message to parents.

Bush announced that he would be creating more charter schools. He then waited to see how parents would react.

The parents were delighted with Bush. They believed that he was expanding the range of schools to which they could send their children. They thanked him profusely.

Bush also kept his eyes on businesspeople.

The businesspeople were delighted. They believed that Bush would be increasing the number of for-profit charter schools. They showed their appreciation by making additional political contributions.

The businesspeople had made another important request: they had asked Bush to promote commercial tests. They were waiting for him to send a signal.

When Bush was ready to provide information, he once again used a dog whistle. He hid the information within a message to parents. He announced that he would require all children to complete a vast battery of commercial educational tests.

Parents were once again pleased with Bush. They believed he was supplying them with important academic data on their children.

Businesspeople also were pleased with Bush. They believed that he would be expanding the market for their products.

* * * * *

Bush won the presidential election of 2001. He succeeded in part because of the skillful manner in which he handled business patrons and parents. He made an impression on Barack Obama, who was a candidate for president eight years later.

Obama was in a position similar to that in which Bush had been: he could not win the election without key groups. He realized that some of these groups would be poring over his educational policies.

Obama was particularly concerned about businesspeople, unionized teachers, and parents. He counted on the businesspeople and the teachers for funding. He counted on the parents for votes.

The businesspeople indicated that they were willing to support the president. However, they expected a payback: they wanted him to continue the Bush-era initiatives affecting for-profit schools and commercial testing.

The teachers were willing to support the president. They also expected a payback: they wanted restrictions on for-profit schools and commercial testing.

Parents were willing to support the president. Many of them still favored more charter schools, including those that were for-profit ventures. However, they now opposed more commercial testing.

After the election, Obama realized that his supporters were waiting for him to reveal his educational priorities. He decided to reveal them within a complex message. He hoped that it would be interpreted differently by each group of supporters.

Obama needed the right opportunity to send his message. He spied one when he was appointing his cabinet: he made one of the appointments into a dog whistle.

Obama selected Arne Duncan as his secretary of education. He then explained why he was the right person to serve in this position.

Obama noted that Duncan had aggressively expanded for-profit schooling and commercial testing when he was the public schools CEO in Chicago. He hoped that businesspeople would hear this information and be pleased.

When the businesspeople listened to the president's message, they were pleased. They anticipated that Duncan would protect their investments.

Although Obama had highlighted the new secretary of education's experiences with businesspeople, he also had highlighted his experiences with professional educators. He had hoped that the teachers would focus on the latter information.

When the teachers listened to the president, they heard the portion of the message that he had aimed at them. However, they also heard the portion that he had aimed at the businesspeople. They were not pleased. They concluded that the president was appeasing business donors at their expense (Rich, 2014).

Obama had been skillful at attracting supporters. He had hoped to be just as skillful at retaining them. However, he recognized he had energized one group of supporters but depressed another. He wondered how his cabinet appointment had affected parents.

* * * * *

Many parents had supported Obama because of a campaign promise to limit commercial testing. They were surprised when he appointed a secretary of education with no commitment to this goal. They wondered whether he was reneging on his promise.

The parents asked their educational questions directly to the president. They expected straightforward answers from him. They were annoyed when they could not get them.

The parents did not give up. They redirected their educational questions to legislators in Congress. They hoped to get candid responses from them.

The legislators wished to handle parents' educational questions in a way that would earn their trust. Although they invariably gave them their full attention, they did not always give them straightforward answers. Like the president, they did not want to reveal their complex and frequently compromising relationships with business firms and their lobbyists.

The legislators realized that answering questions candidly would be damaging. However, they realized that refusing to answer them could be just as damaging. They therefore tried to artfully dodge questions.

One legislator admitted that the parents were upset by his question dodging. He used a sports simile to characterize the different way in which they had begun to treat him.

The legislator once had felt as if he were the trusted coach of a beloved sports team. However, he confessed that he later felt as if he were the anxiety-evoking leader at a "game with 100,000 people in the stands, and every one of them knows what play to call next" (Senator Lamar Alexander, quoted by Rich, 2015).

* * * * *

Tens of thousands of books have been written about children and adolescents at school. How is this one different? What makes it stand out from the others?

This book stands out because of its distinctive content. It highlights the common sense questions that parents have posed about learners. It also highlights the groups that responded to their question, the answers they gave, the rhetoric in which they couched their answers, and their motives.

This book stands out because of its style. It introduces readers to a distinctive analytical approach—the case method. It even contains activities to help them master this approach. These activities are appropriate for persons who are using the case method on their own; they also are appropriate for college students who are using it in their classes.

This book stands out because of its audience. It is aimed at parents and the general public. However, it is just as appropriate for teachers, guidance counselors, principals, superintendents, professors, college students, government leaders, and business leaders.

This book stands out because it is part of a comprehensive series on substantive educational issues. Previous volumes in the series have examined instruction, school administration, and testing (Giordano, 2014, 2015, 2016). This volume examines learners. The next volume will focus on textbooks.

Acknowledgment

When I began this series of books, my editor—Tom Koerner—suggested that I focus it on the questions that parents have raised about schools. I owe him so much for this and countless other instances of sage advice.

Chapter 1

Who Should Take Charge of Educational Funding?

[New York historically has provided modest funding to private schools so that they can] carry out administrative duties the state requires.
—Lisa Fleisher, 2012

[The governor's plan to increase state funding to private schools] would mean a badly needed boost in support for parochial schools.
—Rabbi Dovid Kupchick, quoted by Gormley, 2015

[The governor's funding plan is] a shell game allowing corporations and the super rich to divert tax dollars to elite private schools.
—New York State United Teachers, 2015b

[As to whether my funding plan is the optimal one] there's no right or wrong [answer].
—New York Governor Andrew Cuomo, quoted by Kaplan, 2015

A college administrator concluded that his institution had insufficient funding. A governor concluded that his state provided insufficient funding to private schools. Both leaders announced that they would take charge and recommend controversial solutions.

A CONTRARIAN COLLEGE PRESIDENT

Students had enrolled at Sweet Briar College for over a century. They attended this Virginia school because of its female-only admission policies, sound liberal arts curriculum, nationally accredited degrees, sterling faculty, distinctive academic architecture, smart residence facilities, and vast greens.

Some students had an additional reason for attending Sweet Briar College: they were captivated by its program in equestrian studies. They noted that it comprised distinctive courses on horse showmanship, horse jumping, and horseback hunting. They were impressed that it was supported by a herd of mounts, state-of-the-art stables, a large indoor riding arena, and miles of wooded trails.

Parents were impressed by the college's history of financial stability. Although they conceded that it had a modest-sized endowment, they noted that it had priceless property. They concluded that it was in better financial shape than many other liberal arts schools.

The parents even were impressed by the college's long-serving line of presidents. They noted that it had only two leaders during a recent fifteen-year stretch. They felt reassured when these leaders had described the steps that they were taking to ensure the college's continued operation.

The parents complimented the college's board of governors for the astute leaders that it selected. Although they were advised that this board was appointing an interim president in 2014, many of them did not pay attention. Those who did were unruffled.

The parents remained unruffled even after they discovered that an individual with no experience at the college would serve as the interim president. They assumed that this individual, James Jones, would soon be replaced with a long-term administrator who was committed to preserving and enhancing the college.

Jones occupied a temporary job. Nonetheless, he established an ambitious agenda. He set to work on a comprehensive plan to improve the college.

Jones never finished his plan. He explained that he had to direct all of his energy to a much more important issue: the pending financial collapse of the entire college.

Jones concluded that the collapse would severely harm the students whom the institution served. He added that it also would damage the business firms to which it was indebted.

Jones met with the college's governors. He adjured them to quickly shut down the college and liquidate its assets.

The governors listened carefully to the interim president. They voted to follow his advice and close the school. Moreover, they resolved to close it at the end of the current semester (Stolberg, 2015a, 2015b).

After Jones had left the meeting, he met with faculty members. He told them about the decision to close the school. He stated that this decision was irreversible; he added that it was in the students' best interests.

Jones knew that some faculty members would be absent from the impromptu meeting about the college's fate. He assumed that they would get the information from their colleagues and the media (McKenna, 2015).

Enthusiasts

Some persons supported the interim president. They admired the decisive manner in which he had analyzed a problem, classified it as hopeless, and developed a strategy to restrict the damage.

The enthusiasts stated that they were concerned about students. Although they did not doubt that the school's closing would upset them, they told them that it was in their best interests. They advised them to apply immediately to colleges that were financially stable.

Some of the enthusiasts were convinced that liberal arts colleges had become too eccentric. They believed that they were offering a type of education that no longer made sense. They were especially critical of Sweet Briar because of its high tuition, women-only admission policy, and lavish equestrian program (Treaster, 2015).

Skeptics

The college's governors had not attracted that much notice when they appointed an interim leader. However, they attracted a great deal of attention when they took this individual's recommendation to shudder their college.

Students were flabbergasted when they learned about the interim president's recommendation. They also were offended that he had made it without consulting them.

The students worried that they might not be able to attend colleges that they desired. They explained that transferring to them on short notice was complicated. Even if they were able to transfer to the college of their choice, they likely would receive credit for only a portion of their Sweet Briar coursework (Bouchard, 2015).

Persons who had made donations to Sweet Briar listened to the distraught students. They were upset by the problems that they were describing. However, they had additional reasons to be upset.

Donors had been complaining for years about the manner in which the board of governors had managed the institution's endowment fund. They noted that it had allowed that fund to decline by millions of dollars. They wondered whether it was closing the college in order to occlude injudicious financial practices.

Students, parents, faculty, alumnae, and donors were suspicious when they learned about the closing. They became even more suspicious when they learned about its hasty schedule.

The skeptics had some common sense questions. They directed them to the board of governors. They asked why it hadn't taking steps to resuscitate the college's finances. They asked why it hadn't initiated an emergency fund-raising campaign.

The governors dismissed these questions. After analyzing the college's assets and debts, they had concluded that its finances could not be replenished. They also had concluded that a fund-raising campaign could not succeed (Green, 2015).

The skeptics made their own analysis of the college's assets and debts. They did not share the governors' pessimism. They judged that the college would need only $10 million to remain open. They personally commenced a campaign to raise this amount. They then quickly succeeded.

The skeptics shocked the governors with their financial savvy. They shocked them again with their legal savvy.

The skeptics contacted Virginia's attorney general. They informed him about the bizarre behavior by their board of governors and interim president. They petitioned him to dismiss the governors, fire the interim president, and rescind the order to close the college (Stolberg, 2015b, 2015c).

A CONTRARIAN GOVERNOR

Mario Cuomo had the support of New York's Democrats. He was gratified when they selected him as their gubernatorial candidate during the early 1980s.

Mario Cuomo assembled a talented staff to help win the election. He placed his son, Andrew, in charge.

Andrew Cuomo wanted to make sure that his father had the resources to mount a compelling run for office. He put pressure on liberal-leaning groups to supply money and votes. He assured them that his father would later show his gratitude.

Andrew Cuomo beamed with satisfaction as the campaign progressed. He took a good deal of the credit when his father handily won the general election.

More than two decades later, Andrew Cuomo was still involved in politics. In fact, he hoped to follow his father's path to the governor's mansion.

Cuomo had learned a great deal about politics. He decided to pattern his own campaign after the one that he had orchestrated for his father.

Andrew Cuomo carefully cultivated influential groups. He realized that without them he would have a hard time winning the primary election let alone the general election. He therefore asked the long-standing Democratic supporters to supply him with money and votes. He made a special entreaty to New York's educators, whom he promised to reward later.

Andrew Cuomo won both the primary and general elections in 2010. He then served a four-year term. When he campaigned for another term in office, he triumphed once again.

Cuomo had prevailed in two statewide elections. Since he was not constrained by term limits, he planned to compete in a third gubernatorial election. However, he simultaneously made plans to develop a national political profile.

Cuomo had to widen his political appeal if he were to contend effectively for a national office. He looked to other liberal Democratic politicians for inspiration. He was impressed by Barak Obama, who had used his stance on education to broaden the range of his supporters.

Obama had taken contrarian stances on several key educational issues. As just one example, he had supported charter schools even though his party opposed them.

Charter schools were controversial because of the way in which they were funded and managed. They received funds like public schools even though they were managed more like businesses. They had been resisted by public school teachers because of the money that they siphoned away from public schools.

Cuomo judged that Obama had become more popular because of the steps he had taken to federally fund the nation's charter schools. However, Cuomo already was giving state funds to charter schools. He realized that he would have to do more if he wished to increase his national visibility.

Cuomo had been giving state funds not only to New York's charter schools but also to its private schools. He had inherited this practice. His predecessors had reasoned that New York's private schools deserved modest public funds because they had to carry out state-mandated testing and provide students with health inoculations.

New York's governors had investigated how parents were reacting to their policy of distributing modest state money to private schools. They concluded that those parents with children at private schools supported the policy, which had obvious benefits for them. They noted that those parents who sent their children to public schools also seemed to support the policy, which entailed a relatively modest amount of funding.

Cuomo was ready to make a bold, contrarian recommendation. He would be increasing the amount of state money that he was allocating to private schools. In fact, he would be increasing it substantially (Fleisher, 2012).

Enthusiasts

Andrew Cuomo was not the first governor to recommend substantial state funding for private schools. Jeb Bush had made this recommendation when he was the governor of Florida. Bush then had persuaded his state's legislators to formalize that recommendation into law (Bidwell, 2014; Friedman Foundation for Educational Choice, 2016).

Cuomo envied the publicity that Jeb Bush had generated through his stand on public funding for private schools. He concluded that Bush's stand had helped him develop a reputation as a visionary educational reformer.

Cuomo believed that he could propel his own reputation by backing a proposal similar to the one that Bush had sponsored in Florida. Nonetheless, he recognized that he was in a very different political environment.

Bush had succeeded by convincing Florida's conservative constituency to go along with his proposal. Cuomo had to sell it to a much more liberal constituency.

Cuomo did not believe he would have any difficulty getting support from some constituents. He was sure that he would get it from New York's business community. He noted that this group, even though it was Republican-leaning, had made generous gifts to him during two campaigns.

The business donors had not been naïve: they realized that Cuomo would pursue political initiatives sanctioned by his party. Nonetheless, they still expected some paybacks. They advised him to pursue several initiatives that his party did not endorse. They particularly wanted him to give more state money to private schools (Fleisher, 2012).

The businesspeople were genuinely pleased when Cuomo announced that he supported their request. However, they wanted him to do still more. They encouraged him to look after corporate donors. They explained that he should give them tax credits for the scholarships that they were underwriting at private schools (Schick, 2015).

The businesspeople urged Cuomo to provide tax credits to corporations when they donated money to private schools; they also urged him to provide them to parents when they paid tuition at private schools. They predicted that the corporate leaders and the parents would hail him as a champion of school choice (Schick, 2015).

The businesspeople gave the governor still another reason to follow their advice. They told him that he would ingratiate himself with influential governing boards. They explained that the boards at elite, well-endowed private schools would praise him. They added that the boards at Catholic schools, Jewish yeshivas, and other cash-strapped religious schools also would praise him.

As the businesspeople had predicted, some persons were enthusiastic about the private school tax credit plan. Parents who had children in private schools were especially enthusiastic. They implored Cuomo to put pressure on any senators or assembly members who tried to block the plan (Gormley, 2015; Weaver, 2015).

Republican senators and assembly members extolled the tax credit plan. They stated that it was a pleasure to deal with a visionary Democratic governor. They assured him that his contrarian stance would advance the interests of students at both private schools and public schools (Decker, 2015).

Some Democratic senators and assembly members also extolled the tax credit plan. They agreed with the Republicans that it would help students. However, they conceded that it also would placate some key constituents in their districts (Decker, 2015).

Skeptics

Cuomo listened carefully to the businesspeople. He assured them that he would take their advice.

Cuomo began to aggressively promote his plan. He asked his staff to devise a catchy name for it. He was delighted when they suggested the "Parental Choice in Education" plan (Fertig, 2015).

Cuomo was pleased by the positive reactions of businesspeople to his plan. He also was pleased by the positive reactions of parents who already sent their children to private schools or who were thinking about sending them to private schools.

Cuomo was gratified by the positive reactions of many state legislators. Those legislators who had pledged to support him did. They lauded his efforts to help all students, irrespective of whether they attended public or private schools.

Even though some legislators praised Cuomo, others were critical. His fellow Democrats were the most critical. They noted that he was sponsoring a plan that was incompatible with his party's state and national priorities.

The skeptical legislators challenged the governor's claim that he was looking out for students. They suggested that he was looking after his own political interests. They scolded him for acting unethically.

The skeptics noted that the governor was allocating state revenue to religious schools. They reminded him that Jeb Bush, who had tried to make this type of allocation in Florida, had been checked in the courts. They warned Cuomo that he was acting illegally (Bidwell, 2014; Friedman Foundation for Educational Choice, 2016).

The skeptical legislators noted that some tax credits would go to wealthy donors who sent their children to well-endowed private schools. They advised Cuomo that he would be ridiculed for pandering to these donors (Fleisher, 2012; Kaplan, 2015; Schick, 2015).

The skeptical legislators had still another reason that they were upset with Cuomo. They reminded him that he had made a campaign promise to public school teachers. They were sure that he would be rebuked by them.

The teachers did rebuke Cuomo. They were certain that his plan to allocate more money to private schools would reduce the amount that was available to public schools; they also were certain that it would harm the students at their schools (Decker, 2015; New York State United Teachers, 2015b).

The teachers asked journalists to take their side in the dispute with the governor. They were delighted when they joined them. They were even more delighted when they persuaded many parents to join them.

The teachers, journalists, and parents were a powerful coalition. They told Cuomo that New York already had serious educational problems. They did not believe that his plan would solve any of them. To the contrary, they predicted that it actually would create more problems. They implored him to reconsider it.

Cuomo would not back down. Although he did acknowledge that some problems were inevitable, he stated that those problems were so complicated that they did not have right or wrong solutions.

Cuomo tried to illustrate the complexity of the educational problems with which he was dealing. He conceded that his tax credit plan would reduce the revenue that the state collected. However, he quickly added that it would expand parental school choice. He contended that this tradeoff was worthwhile (Kaplan, 2015).

EXAMINING QUESTIONS POSED TO CONTRARIAN LEADERS

An administrator examined the funding at his college. Convinced that it was hopelessly insufficient, he recommended that the college close. A governor examined state funding to private schools. Convinced that it was grossly insufficient, he recommended a substantial increase. Although both leaders acknowledged that they were making contrarian recommendations, they insisted that they were making them because of their concern for students.

Activity 1.1

The presidents at Sweet Briar College had all come to a predictable conclusion: the school could best help students by continuing to operate. How did groups respond?

Table 1.1 identifies two groups at the college: the board of governors and the students.

Complete the table by indicating the ways in which the groups responded. You can use symbols.

Use the symbol – if the groups expressed low confidence. Use the symbol ± for moderate confidence and the symbol + for high confidence. As a final step, explain the bases for the symbols that you selected.

You can rely on the information in this chapter, additional information, or the information cited in the references. If you are reading this chapter with colleagues, you can confer with them.

Table 1.1. Presidents Recommend That Their College Continue Operating

Groups	Response*	Explanation
Board of Governors		
Students		

*– Low
± Moderate
+ High

Activity 1.2

An interim president at Sweet Briar College came to a contrarian conclusion: the school could best help students by ceasing to operate. How did groups respond?

Table 1.2 identifies two groups at the college: the board of governors and the students.

Complete the table by indicating the ways in which the groups responded. You can use symbols.

Use the symbol – if the groups expressed low confidence. Use the symbol ± for moderate confidence and the symbol + for high confidence. As a final step, explain the bases for the symbols that you selected.

Table 1.2. An Interim President Recommends That His College Cease Operating

Groups	Response*	Explanation
Board of Governors		
Students		

*– Low
± Moderate
+ High

Activity 1.3

Recent governors of New York had all come to a predictable conclusion: the state could best help students by giving modest funds to private schools. How did groups respond?

Table 1.3 identifies two groups: the parents of students in private schools and the parents of students in public schools.

Complete the table by indicating the ways in which the groups responded. You can use symbols.

Use the symbol – if the groups expressed low confidence. Use the symbol ± for moderate confidence and the symbol + for high confidence. As a final step, explain the bases for the symbols that you selected.

Table 1.3. New York's Governors Recommend Modest Public Funds for Private Schools

Groups	Response*	Explanation
Parents—Private Schools		
Parents—Public Schools		

*– Low
± Moderate
+ High

Activity 1.4

Governor Andrew Cuomo came to a contrarian conclusion: New York could best help students by giving significantly more funds to private schools. How did groups respond?

Table 1.4 identifies two groups: the parents of students in private schools and the parents of students in public schools.

Complete the table by indicating the ways in which the groups responded. You can use symbols.

Use the symbol – if the groups expressed low confidence. Use the symbol ± for moderate confidence and the symbol + for high confidence. As a final step, explain the bases for the symbols that you selected.

Table 1.4. A New York Governor Recommends Substantial Public Funds for Private Schools

Groups	Response*	Explanation
Parents—Private Schools		
Parents—Public Schools		

*− Low
± Moderate
+ High

SUMMARY

An administrator was concerned about the funding at his college. A governor was concerned about the funding that his state provided to private schools. In both cases, they made contrarian proposals. In both cases, they insisted that they were making them to help students.

Chapter 2

Who Should Take Charge of School Menus?

> Bad nutrition can get in the way of ability to learn.
> —Congressman George Miller, quoted by Nelson, 2014

> Improving child nutrition is the focal point of the Healthy, Hunger-Free Kids Act.
> —U.S. Department of Agriculture, 2014

> [Take my cafeteria meal] to the Superintendent and tell him to eat it.
> —High School Student Kaytlin Shelton, as quoted in "Family's Anger," 2014

> Teach your child that he is in charge of what goes into his body [at school].
> —Childhood Feeding Specialists Katja Rowell & Jenny McGlothlin, 2015

Executives expressed concern about how well their restaurant menus suited patrons. Politicians expressed a similar concern about school menus. Both groups pledged to take charge and change the menus.

CORPORATE EXECUTIVES

Olive Garden restaurants appeared during the 1980s. They were immensely popular.

Executives at the Darden Corporation operated Olive Garden restaurants. Although they were responsible for several other chains, they realized that none of them attracted as many patrons as their Italian-themed restaurants. They opened more of them as quickly they could.

Persons who visited Olive Garden restaurants were impressed. They took notice of the jumbo-sized entrees. They were struck by the never-ending supplies of breadsticks. They were eager to return.

The Darden executives were pleased with the culinary formula that they had discovered. They assumed that they would use it indefinitely.

Customers later exhibited a change of attitude. They began to tire of the Olive Gardens. They made their displeasure evident by staying away.

Like customers, investors exhibited a change in attitude. Some of them had purchased Darden's stock because it paid generous dividends. They became disgruntled when declining patronage caused declining dividends. They showed their displeasure by dumping their stock.

Professional observers tried to comprehend what was happening at the Olive Gardens. Some of them believed that they understood the reason for the declining patronage. They concluded that consumers had lost interest in the meals that were generically prepared. They explained that they now preferred meals comprising small portions of authentically prepared items. They euphemistically stated that they had developed small-plate palates (Choi, 2014).

Many investors agreed with the professional observers. They urged the executives to take charge of their menus. They wanted them to offer small-plate options to customers. They also wanted them to provide fewer breadsticks to them.

Enthusiasts

The Darden executives did take charge of their menus: they made the changes for which investors were clamoring. However, they soon detected an inadvertent consequence.

Many patrons did not approve of the changes. They preferred to leave the restaurants as they formerly had—with their stomachs bulging.

When the executives realized that they were alienating consumers, they searched for a way to placate them. However, they were not sure how to win them back without angering investors.

The executives decided to act cautiously. They told consumers that they would stand by their recent changes. However, they tried to give them a convincing rationale. They told them that Olive Garden had to join a national trend in which restaurants were providing smaller portions.

The executives waited to see how consumers would react to their explanation. They were distressed when they continued to avoid their restaurants. They were even more distressed when this behavior led to an even steeper plunge in profits.

The executives admitted that they needed a different strategy to save their restaurant chain. They turned to marketers for advice.

The marketers quickly came up with a suggestion. They wished to implement a high-profile promotion. They would sell special bargain passes, which they referred to as Pasta Passes.

Individuals would have to pay $100 for a Pasta Pass. They then could visit an unlimited number of Olive Garden restaurants and consume unlimited amounts of pasta for seven weeks. They even could bring guests by upgrading to a $300 Pasta Pass (Choi, 2015).

Skeptics

Business analysts had complained for years about Darden restaurants' declining income. They had urged the executives to take steps to arrest it. They were attentive when the corporation's executives announced changes.

Business analysts studied the steps that the corporation's executives had authorized. For example, they examined their redesigned menu and new breadstick policy. Some of them were impressed. They truly believed that they were on the verge of increasing their patronage (Drum, 2014; Weissmann, 2014).

Not all analysts had confidence in the Olive Garden's new menu and breadstick policy. Some felt that the Darden executives had been maladroit. They doubted that they had addressed the real reasons that consumers were avoiding their restaurants (Vara, 2014).

Other business analysts reached a different conclusion about the executives. They suspected that they had been devious rather than maladroit. They did not believe that they had been making changes to lure back patrons. They concluded that they had been making them for very different reasons.

The critics disdained Olive Garden's new menu and breadstick policy. They were even more disdainful of the Pasta Passes. After pointing out that only several thousand of them had been released, they concluded that they never were intended to change customers' attitudes (Quirk, 2015).

The critics believed that the executives had been making changes to menus in order to conceal the changes that they were making to leases. They noted they had split their company into two units: one that was responsible for operating and another for leasing. They explained that they could make this split because they controlled the buildings in which Olive Garden restaurants operated and the land on which those buildings were constructed.

The critics believed that the executives had a good reason for reorganizing. They were certain that they were about to raise their leases and bring in more cash.

Investors approved of the executives' plan. They assumed that the leasing unit would flourish, generate profits, and gather enough money to pay dividends.

Consumers did not approve of the executives' plan. Even though most of them were unaware of its details, they still could detect the effects. They noted that the restaurant managers, who had to pay more money for their leases, had less to pay for skilled staff, modern equipment, and high-quality food (Dayen, 2014).

The executives tried to reason with disgruntled consumers. They insisted that they were making changes to benefit them. They pleaded with them to return to their restaurants.

The consumers remained skeptical. They did not believe that the executives had been trying to enhance their dining experiences. They declared that they had no intention of returning (Dayen, 2014).

SCHOOL CAFETERIA MANAGERS

School cafeteria managers had difficult jobs. They had to prepare meals for hundreds of students. They had to make sure that they were nutritious, appetizing, and affordable.

The cafeteria managers were under severe financial pressure. They had limited budgets to staff and operate their facilities. They readily acknowledged that they needed assistance.

The cafeteria managers received assistance from the federal government. They were provided with money and food. They used these resources to subsidize their operations; they also used them to give either low-priced or completely free meals to students.

The cafeteria managers had begun to receive federal assistance during the 1940s. They then continued to receive it for decades.

Politicians took credit for the school cafeteria subsidies. They bragged that they helped students grow physically and perform academically.

The politicians routinely reauthorized funding for the school cafeterias. In fact, they frequently increased the amount. They eventually were awarding $16 billion a year ("Federal School Nutrition Programs," 2015).

Businesspeople were enthusiastic about the school lunch programs. They acknowledged that they benefitted students. However, they also acknowledged that they helped the individuals and corporations involved in farming and food processing. They lobbied the politicians to ensure that certain produce and food items were sent to the schools.

Although the politicians assisted school cafeteria managers, they did not tell them which meals to serve. They expected them to plan them on their own. When they sent them wheat flour, they allowed them to decide whether they would use it for bread, tortillas, biscuits, or pizza. They also allowed them to select the recipes that they would follow.

The cafeteria managers were trained, qualified, and ready to make decisions about the items on menus. They were comfortable with the way the politicians treated them.

The cafeteria managers wanted to prepare items that were nutritious and tasty. They paid attention to dietary guidelines. They also paid careful attention to the way that students reacted to their food.

The cafeteria managers noted that students lustily ate some food items. They identified pizza, hamburgers, and tacos as dishes that they especially loved. Consequently, they served these selections regularly.

Enthusiasts

School cafeteria managers had been excited when Barrack Obama was elected president in 2008. They noted that he had campaigned on a pledge to reduce childhood obesity. They wholeheartedly supported this goal.

The president had a simple plan: he challenged children to eat healthy foods and exercise. He enlisted his charismatic wife to assist him.

The school cafeteria managers extolled Obama's plan. They encouraged their professional association, the School Nutrition Association, to endorse it.

The president valued the publicity from the School Nutrition Association's endorsement. Nonetheless, he wished to take additional steps to ensure that his plan was rigorously implemented. He asked federal legislators to give it a name, legally codify it, and assign it to a federal agency.

The legislators came up with a catchy name for the plan: the Healthy, Hunger-Free Kids Act. They codified school lunch regulations within it. They specified that the Department of Agriculture should ensure that the schools were following the regulations (U.S. Department of Agriculture, 2014).

After the new federal school lunch legislation was enacted, the cafeteria managers examined it carefully. They were surprised. They had not expected it to be so doctrinaire. They realized that it had removed their menus from their control.

The cafeteria managers were adjured to adjust the way that they were serving food items. For example, they were directed to serve fresh fruits and vegetables frequently. They were warned to avoid milk that had more than 1 percent fat, bread that had less than 50 percent whole grain, foods that had trans fats added to them, or any meals that exceeded precisely prescribed calorie limits (U.S. Department of Agriculture, 2014).

The cafeteria managers were advised to follow the new regulations. They were warned that they otherwise would lose their federal school lunch funding (Aubrey, 2014; Brody, 2014).

Skeptics

Students were not happy with the new school lunch menus. They complained that they no longer were able to enjoy their favorite foods.

Students were irked by items that had been removed from the cafeteria menus. They also were irked by the portion sizes of those that remained. They stated that food items were too small to satisfy their hunger ("Family's Anger," 2014).

The students had another complaint about food items: they had become less savory. They initially compensated by sprinkling salt from the shakers on lunchroom tables. However, they were told that the shakers had to go because of government-imposed salt restrictions. They then had to get salt from home and sneak it into school ("Government Food Flight," 2015).

Students wished to express their feelings about the new cafeteria food. Some of them were polite: they shunned the food and began to bring items from home instead. Others were theatrical: they made a show of tossing the food uneaten into trash cans (Cheshire, 2014; Evich, 2014).

Childhood eating specialists became aware of the turmoil in the school lunchrooms. They were extremely upset.

The eating specialists blamed politicians for the manner in which they had made the lunchroom changes. Although they conceded that they may have had good intentions, they believed that they should have been more sophisticated.

The eating specialists wished that the politicians had been more attentive to all of the factors that contributed to healthy eating habits. These included local culinary culture, religious restrictions on diets, medical restrictions on diets, and parental attitudes toward foods (Rowell & McGlothlin, 2015).

The eating specialists were upset with school administrators as well as politicians. They believed that the school administrators were compounding the school lunchroom problems.

The eating specialists were chagrinned when school administrators forbade students from leaving the cafeterias until they had eaten all of the items on their lunch trays. They warned that they were undermining rather than reinforcing healthy eating habits.

The eating specialists urged parents to rebel. They equipped them with practical strategies. For example, they suggested that they give children cards to hand to pushy lunchroom monitors.

> Please don't ask [my child] to eat more or different foods than she/he wants. Please let her eat as much as she wants of any of the foods I pack, in any order, even if she eats nothing or only dessert. (Rowell & McGlothlin, 2015)

The cafeteria managers were jarred when rebellious parents challenged their new menus. They responded defensively: they stated that they had made changes to the menus only because they were concerned about health and learning.

The parents were not placated. They were not convinced that the cafeteria managers had given them the true reason for the changes. They believed that they had been pressured by the government to make changes or forfeit federal assistance.

The parents urged the managers to take charge of their cafeterias. They explained that they should make the food more savory, serve it in larger portions, and return student favorites to the menu.

Many of the school cafeteria managers belonged to the School Nutrition Association. They asked Leah Schmidt, the president of this organization, to convey their concerns to the U.S. Department of Agriculture.

Schmidt noted that school cafeteria managers initially had supported the regulations. She stated that they had changed their minds after they had observed how students and parents were reacting.

Schmidt had an unsettling question for federal bureaucrats. She asked if they were going to accept responsibility for the mountains of food that were ending up in school trash bins (Fischer, 2014; Hope, 2014).

President Obama learned that the cafeteria managers had reversed their stance on his school lunch regulations. He was not pleased. Quite to the contrary, he was furious.

Obama blasted the cafeteria managers. He noted that they were members of an organization that received contributions from large food corporations. He accused them of succumbing to pressure from those corporations.

President Obama blamed the cafeteria managers for succumbing to pressure from another influential group—congressional conservatives. He was sure that the conservatives had political reasons for opposing the new school lunch regulations (Evich, 2014; Lochhead, 2014).

The cafeteria managers stood up to the president. They told him that they had not changed their minds about his regulations because of corporations or politicians. They stated that they had changed them because of the damage to schoolchildren (Linnell-Olsen, 2015).

The cafeteria managers told the president that they had one more reason for changing their minds about the new regulations. They noted that they could not stay within their budgets because the regulations were so prescriptive.

The managers challenged the president to increase the budget for the food that he was prescribing. They wanted him to cover their actual costs. They warned that he otherwise might force them to opt out of his program (Donegan, 2014; Nelson, 2014).

EXAMINING QUESTIONS ABOUT MOTIVES

Restaurant executives contended that they made changes because they were concerned about patrons. However, they were disparaged for pandering to investors. When school cafeteria managers made the same contention, they were chastised for pandering to politicians.

Activity 2.1

Olive Garden's executives attempted to raise enough money to operate their restaurants and pay corporate dividends. They relied on a simple culinary formula: colossal-sized portions and endless breadsticks. How did groups respond?

Table 2.1 identifies two groups: investors and consumers.

Complete the table by indicating the ways in which the groups responded to the executives. You can use symbols.

Use the symbol – if the groups expressed low confidence in them. Use the symbol ± for moderate confidence and the symbol + for high confidence. As a final step, explain the bases for the symbols that you selected.

You can rely on the information in this chapter, additional information, or the information cited in the references. If you are reading this chapter with colleagues, you can confer with them.

Table 2.1. Restaurant Executives Provide Colossal-Sized Portions and Endless Breadsticks

Groups	Response*	Explanation
Investors		
Consumers		

*– Low
± Moderate
+ High

Activity 2.2

Olive Garden's executives were disappointed with the money that they were raising. They began to use a new culinary formula: smaller portions and fewer breadsticks. How did groups respond?

Table 2.2 identifies two groups: investors and consumers.

Complete the table by indicating the ways in which the groups responded to the executives. You can use symbols.

Use the symbol – if the groups expressed low confidence in them. Use the symbol ± for moderate confidence and the symbol + for high confidence. As a final step, explain the bases for the symbols that you selected.

Table 2.2. Restaurant Executives Downsize Portions and Limit Breadsticks

Groups	Response*	Explanation
Investors		
Consumers		

*– Low
± Moderate
+ High

Activity 2.3

After they had reconfigured menus, the Olive Garden's executives were still disappointed with the money that they were raising. They therefore reconfigured their leases. How did groups respond?

Table 2.3 identifies two groups: investors and consumers.

Complete the table by indicating the ways in which the groups responded to the executives. You can use symbols.

Use the symbol – if the groups expressed low confidence in them. Use the symbol ± for moderate confidence and the symbol + for high confidence. As a final step, explain the bases for the symbols that you selected.

Table 2.3. Restaurant Executives Reconfigure Leasing Arrangements

Groups	Response*	Explanation
Investors		
Consumers		

*– Low
± Moderate
+ High

Activity 2.4

School cafeteria managers attempted to serve meals that students would consume and enjoy. They relied on a simple culinary formula: large portions of not-always-healthy foods. How did groups respond?

Table 2.4 identifies two groups: politicians and parents of schoolchildren.

Complete the table by indicating the ways in which the groups responded to the managers. You can use symbols.

Use the symbol – if the groups expressed low confidence in them. Use the symbol ± for moderate confidence and the symbol + for high confidence. As a final step, explain the bases for the symbols that you selected.

Table 2.4. School Cafeteria Managers Provide Large Portions of Not-Always-Healthy Foods

Groups	Response*	Explanation
Politicians		
Parents		

*– Low
± Moderate
+ High

Activity 2.5

School cafeteria managers were pressured to use a federally mandated culinary formula: small portions of healthy foods. How did groups respond?

Table 2.5 identifies two groups: politicians and parents of schoolchildren.

Complete the table by indicating the ways in which the groups responded to the managers. You can use symbols.

Use the symbol – if the groups expressed low confidence in them. Use the symbol ± for moderate confidence and the symbol + for high confidence. As a final step, explain the bases for the symbols that you selected.

Table 2.5. School Cafeteria Managers Provide Small Portions of Healthy Foods

Groups	Response*	Explanation
Politicians		
Parents		

*– Low
± Moderate
+ High

Activity 2.6

The school cafeteria managers were disappointed with the way students responded to smaller portions and healthier foods. They campaigned to regain control of menus. How did groups respond?

Table 2.6 identifies two groups: politicians and parents of schoolchildren.

Complete the table by indicating the ways in which the groups responded to the managers. You can use symbols.

Use the symbol – if the groups expressed low confidence in them. Use the symbol ± for moderate confidence and the symbol + for high confidence. As a final step, explain the bases for the symbols that you selected.

Table 2.6. School Cafeteria Managers Campaign against Federal Lunch Regulations

Groups	Response*	Explanation
Politicians		
Parents		

*– Low
± Moderate
+ High

SUMMARY

Restaurant executives and school cafeteria managers contended that they were making changes because they were concerned about their patrons. However, both groups were accused of being disingenuous.

Chapter 3

Who Should Take Charge of Students' Smartphones?

[I am banning smartphones because] schools are for learning.
—New York City Mayor Michael Bloomberg, quoted by Cardwell & Hu, 2006

I'm suspicious of the arguments that the mayor . . . put forward as the reasons for [his school smartphone] prohibition.
—Former New York Civil Liberties Union Director Norman Siegel, quoted by Gootman, 2006b

[The mayor should not have banned smartphones because they] are an important way for parents and students to communicate.
—New York City Council Member Bill de Blasio, quoted in "Cell Phones Should," 2008

Our policy of no electronic devices during the school day was inconsistent with societal norms.
—High School Principal Kate Long, quoted in "Should We Allow," 2011

Telecommunications executives initially allowed marketers to design corporate smartphone policies. An urban mayor initially allowed educators to design school smartphone policies. However, they later changed their minds, personally took charge of the policies, and redesigned them.

EXECUTIVES ALTER CORPORATE SMARTPHONE POLICIES

Telecommunications executives wished to attract new customers to their smartphone service plans. They asked marketers to assist them.

The marketers were sure that they could help. They recommended service plans in which customers could download unlimited network data for a fixed price. They made this recommendation to the executives at several corporations, including AT&T, Verizon, and T-Mobile.

The telecommunications executives followed the marketers' advice. They were pleased when they then sold millions of unlimited data service plans. They assumed that they would sell these types of plans indefinitely.

The executives at AT&T and Verizon soon changed their minds. They judged that they would be making much more money by selling smartphone plans that had limits on data. They explained that they intended to charge customers extra fees whenever they exceeded those limits.

The T-Mobile executives believed that their competitors at AT&T and Verizon had been unwise. They predicted that they would alienate customers. They feared that they even might make some of T-Mobile customers anxious about the long-term prospect for their company's plans.

The executives at T-Mobile wished to reassure customers. They declared that they would continue to make unlimited data plans available to them. In fact, they would make them available to customers who left other carriers to join their network.

The T-Mobile executives expected to keep their current subscribers. Furthermore, they expected to attract some new ones. They believed that they then would increase their corporate profits and stock values (Keating, 2015).

The executives did not achieve their goals. They had fewer customers than their competitors; they also had declining profits and sinking stock values. They blamed their marketers (Chen, 2015).

Enthusiasts

The executives resolved to personally take charge of T-Mobile's smartphone data plans. They stated that they still would be selling plans with unlimited data. However, they would modify them.

The executives announced that they would be charging higher fees to persons who purchased unlimited data plans but who then used unreasonable amounts of data. They warned that they might even ban these persons from their network.

The executives wondered how groups would respond to the changes that they had made. They were concerned about three groups: investors, customers, and journalists.

The executives were sure that investors would be pleased with the changes. They had been under pressure from them to adopt data usage policies similar to those of their competitors.

The executives were less sure how customers would react to the changes. They believed that many of them had subscribed to T-Mobile precisely because of the way their current smartphone plans were structured.

The executives tried to calm customers about the changes. They told them that they were unlikely to observe any negative repercussions from them. They added that they actually should enjoy faster processing speeds after heavy data users were barred from the network.

The executives had one more group about which they were concerned—journalists. They cared about them because of the influence they exerted on stockholders and customers. They hoped that they would be supportive (Welch, 2015).

Skeptics

Not all persons had confidence in the T-Mobile executives. Some were skeptical of them.

The skeptics discovered that the executives were using special software to monitor the data usage of customers. They wanted to know their motives.

The executives acknowledged that they were monitoring their customers. However, they stated that they were interested in only those individuals who were abusing their service plans. They maintained that they had no interest in the others ("Stopping Network Abusers," 2015).

The skeptics asked the executives to estimate the percentage of T-Mobile subscribers who were abusing service plans. They were shocked when they conjectured that the number was less than one in every ten thousand subscribers.

The skeptics wanted to know why the executives were focusing so intently on such a small problem. They doubted that their efforts were cost-effective. They also doubted that they would free up enough bandwidth to increase downloading speeds.

The skeptics criticized the executives not just for the actions they had taken but even the rhetoric they employed. They mocked them for using the term "unlimited data usage" to identify plans that now had strictly limited data usage (Chen, 2015).

The executives were disconcerted when customers posed challenging questions. However, they were even more disconcerted when journalists repeated their questions. They feared that the journalists could attract a large audience and tarnish their corporation's public image.

The executives had requested that journalists help them deal with surly customers. However, they realized that many of them did not wish to cooperate. They therefore decided to ignore the journalists.

The executives stated that they did not need the journalist to help them answer the questions that customers were posing. They would personally answer them. They created a special website on which they posted and responded to questions.

The executives responded to a question about whether they were changing smartphone policies in order to extract more money from subscribers. They stated that they were making the changes solely to look after their subscribers' best interests ("Stopping Network Abusers," 2015).

POLITICIANS ALTER SCHOLASTIC SMARTPHONE POLICIES

Michael Bloomberg had an enviable reputation. He was a savvy entrepreneur, the director of a vast commercial empire, and one of the richest persons in the United States.

Bloomberg was pleased with the attention that he received from his business peers. However, he still was ambitious. He hoped to get more attention from the general public.

Bloomberg calculated that a career in politics would help him get the attention he craved. He detected a prime opportunity: he would compete in the 2001 election for mayor of New York City.

During his campaign, Bloomberg was asked about the changes that he would make as mayor. Although he declined to provide details, he pledged to release them if he were to win the election.

Bloomberg did win the election. As he had promised, he then began to reveal the goals that he had set.

Journalists were eager to examine Bloomberg's goals. They were particularly intrigued by those that involved the city's schools. They reminded him that he had never had any personal contact with the schools. They asked him how he intended to improve institutions with which he was completely inexperienced.

Bloomberg was annoyed by the journalist. Nonetheless, he realized that he had to be careful with them. He did not underestimate their skill at making him appear incompetent.

Bloomberg was particularly worried that the journalists would make parents anxious. He therefore personally reassured the parents. He promised them that he would employ a balanced, patient, common sense approach to the schools. He added that he would solicit their advice and follow it (*New York Times* Editorial Board, 2009).

At the beginning of his first term, Bloomberg kept his word: he systematically gave parents chances to express their thoughts about the schools. He was gratified when the parents reciprocated and gave him high approval ratings.

Bloomberg later became impatient about the amount of time that he was spending to make even minor scholastic changes. He was eager to make substantive changes. He therefore altered the way he was handling parents.

Bloomberg had succeeded in business by being decisive, quick, and bold. He wished to adopt a similar managerial style in the schools. Nonetheless, he did not wish to appear autocratic. He had to come up with a rationale for his new take-charge managerial style.

Bloomberg announced that he was about to move forward and make dramatic changes in the schools. He explained that he could move forward because he already had listened to the advice that parents had for him.

Bloomberg paraphrased the parents' advice. He stated that they wanted scholastic options. He had a common sense solution for this problem: he would provide more charter schools (New York City Charter School Center, 2015).

Bloomberg identified another change that parents wanted him to make. He contended that they desperately wanted more information about their children's academic progress. He explained that they were frustrated by the scant scholastic data that they were receiving.

Bloomberg had a common sense solution for the second problem. He would require students to complete more commercial scholastic tests. He then would share the results with parents (Fertig, 2013).

The parents had mixed reactions to the mayor's two proposals. Although many of them supported the push for more charter schools, they did not support the push for more testing. They were surprised when the mayor charged ahead with both initiatives.

When he began a second term in 2006, Bloomberg realized that journalists and constituents were waiting for him to announce whether he had modified his educational goals. He stated that he still was concerned about school choice and testing. However, he added that he had become concerned about student misbehavior as well.

Bloomberg was convinced that students were misbehaving more than ever. He came up with a surprisingly simple explanation: they were abusing their smartphones.

Blomberg did concede that students used their smartphones to transmit and receive critically important messages. He acknowledged that they felt safer and probably were safer because they used smartphones. Nonetheless, he was sure that they primarily used them for trivial purposes, such as entertainment.

During his initial term, Bloomberg had made educators responsible for school smartphone policies. He reasoned that the educators were in a good position to look after the students' interests. He therefore listened to them when they stated that the teachers and administrators at individual schools should regulate smartphones.

Bloomberg later regretted his decision. He concluded that he had placed too much trust in the educators. He believed that their lenient smartphone policies had fostered misbehavior (Gootman, 2006b).

Bloomberg announced that he no longer would be taking educators' advice about students' smartphones. He personally was taking charge: he was banning smartphones from every school in the city.

Bloomberg predicted that his ban would reduce disruptive behaviors. He also predicted that it would improve learning and increase test scores (Gootman, 2006a).

Enthusiasts

Bloomberg had sponsored three key educational initiatives in the city. He initially increased the number of charter schools. He then expanded commercial scholastic testing. He later banned students' smartphones.

Bloomberg was aware that his city's public schools had fierce critics. He hoped that these critics would support all three of his educational initiatives.

Bloomberg noted that the school critics had been championing charter schools and commercial tests for decades. He therefore was sure that they would commend him for his first two initiatives. He was less certain about the way they would react to his smartphone ban.

The school critics were cautious about the mayor's educational initiatives. They were concerned about their impact on public school spending, which they believed was excessive. They carefully calculated the costs associated with each proposal.

The school critics realized that substantial spending would be needed for more charter schools and more commercial tests. Nonetheless, they also realized that this spending would be much less than that which public school advocates had been requesting. They pointed out that the school advocates wanted money to hire additional instructors, upgrade antiquated technology, and replaced obsolete learning materials (Giordano 2012b, 2014, 2015, 2016).

The school critics concluded that the mayor's plans to increase the number of charter schools and expand commercial testing, even though they would be costly, were relative bargains. They therefore supported them. They were even more supportive of the smartphone ban, which did not require any funds whatsoever.

Bloomberg believed that some New York City teachers and administrators disapproved of smartphones. He was sure that they shared his conviction that the devices hampered discipline, reduced learning, and suppressed test scores. Nonetheless, he realized that they were a small minority. He anticipated opposition from the majority of them (Cardwell & Hu, 2006).

Before he had announced his phone ban, Bloomberg had deliberated about the ways in which school critics and educators would react. He had expected strong support from the school critics but firm opposition from the educators.

However, he had failed to consider how another important group would react—the city's many independent entrepreneurs.

The entrepreneurs were excited about the mayor's smartphone ban. In fact, they showed greater enthusiasm than the school critics. They were enthusiastic because they detected an opportunity to make money.

The entrepreneurs predicted that the smartphone ban would disconcert students. They explained that it would make them fear that their phones would be confiscated by zealous teachers.

The entrepreneurs had a way to restore calm. They set up curbside stands near schools. They told students that those who paid a daily fee could check their phones as they were entering school and then retrieve them as they were leaving (Kiema, 2015).

Bloomberg wondered how journalists would cover his push to ban smartphones. He had been pleased with the way they had covered his earlier pushes to expand charter schools and increase testing. He noted that they had given him extensive publicity. He hoped that they would give him comparable publicity for his newest educational initiative.

Bloomberg was disappointed with the journalists. He realized that they were paying hardly any attention to his ban. However, he did not give up on them. He hoped that they would change their minds.

The journalists eventually did change their minds and begin to cover the smartphone ban. However, they concentrated almost exclusively on the way the ban had benefitted local entrepreneurs.

Skeptics

Bloomberg insisted that he had restricted smartphones at the behest of parents. He explained that the parents originally had demanded more charter schools and more commercial tests. They later demanded fewer smartphones.

The parents disagreed with the mayor. Although many of them had supported his charter school initiative, few had supported his testing initiative. None of them had supported his smartphone initiative.

The parents noted that they had to be able to contact their children during the school day. They explained that they had to give them important information about transportation, meals, homecare, weather, and family emergencies. They wanted to contact them in a way that was direct, easy, and foolproof: they wanted to use smartphones (Gootman, 2006a, 2006b).

The parents also wanted their children to have opportunities to contact them during the school day. They contended that they should be able to contact them when they were lonely, fearful, or simply disconcerted. They emphasized that these feelings, which might go undetected by busy teachers and principals, were critically important to children and their parents.

The parents even challenged the mayor on the reasons that he had given for imposing the ban. They doubted that he was trying to alter children's behavior, learning, and test scores. They suspected that he instead was trying to enhance his own reputation (Shapiro, 2015).

As for students, they had little respect for their mayor. They viewed him as a bureaucrat who did not have a clue about the importance of smartphones to their lives. They did not want him to separate them from their phones.

The students became even more annoyed after their peers had discussed the ban with them. They discovered that some of them were at schools that were zealously enforcing the ban while others were at schools that were ignoring it.

Many students rebelled against the ban. They smuggled their phones into school and used them secretly. Some did not even turn off the alarms: they downloaded high-pitched tones that they could hear but that adults with less acute hearing could not detect (Vitello, 2006).

Many teachers sided with their rebellious students. They agreed that they needed smartphones to stay connected and safe (Atkeson, 2014).

The teachers had additional reasons for supporting their students. They noted that they could use their smartphones to collaborate on classroom projects, complete homework, and conduct research. They contended that these activities, which benefitted them currently at school, would help them later in the workplace ("Cell Phones Should Not," 2008; "Should We Allow," 2011).

EXAMINING DISINGENUOUS ANSWERS TO QUESTIONS

T-Mobile executives initially followed marketers' advice on smartphones. They reasoned that the marketers were in a good position to look after customers' interests. When they later changed their minds, they stated that executives were in a better position to look after customers.

A New York City mayor initially followed educators' advice on smartphones. He reasoned that the educators were in a good position to look after students' interests. When he later changed his mind, he insisted that he was in a better position to look after students.

Activity 3.1

T-Mobile executives initially took marketers advice about smartphone plans. They reasoned that the marketers were in a good position to look after customers' interests. How did groups respond?

Table 3.1 identifies two groups: T-Mobile customers and journalists.

Complete the table by indicating the ways in which the groups responded to the executives. You can use symbols.

Who Should Take Charge of Students' Smartphones? 33

Use the symbol – if the groups expressed low confidence in them. Use the symbol ± for moderate confidence and the symbol + for high confidence. As a final step, explain the bases for the symbols that you selected.

You can rely on the information in this chapter, additional information, or the information cited in the references. If you are reading this chapter with colleagues, you can confer with them.

Table 3.1. T-Mobile Executives Take Marketers' Advice about Smartphone Plans

Groups	Response*	Explanation
Customers		
Journalists		

*– Low
± Moderate
+ High

Activity 3.2

T-Mobile executives later ignored marketers' advice about smartphone plans. Asserting that they were in the best position to look after customers, they announced that they personally would make decisions about the plans. How did groups respond?

Table 3.2 identifies two groups: T-Mobile customers and journalists.

Complete the table by indicating the ways in which the groups responded to the executives. You can use symbols.

Use the symbol – if the groups expressed low confidence in them. Use the symbol ± for moderate confidence and the symbol + for high confidence. As a final step, explain the bases for the symbols that you selected.

Table 3.2. T-Mobile Executives Ignore Marketers' Advice about Smartphone Plans

Groups	Response*	Explanation
Customers		
Journalists		

*– Low
± Moderate
+ High

Activity 3.3

New York City's mayor initially took educators' advice about students' smartphones. He reasoned that the educators were in a good position to look after students' interests. How did groups respond?

Table 3.3 identifies two New York City groups: teachers and parents.

Complete the table by indicating the ways in which the groups responded to the mayor. You can use symbols.

Use the symbol – if the groups expressed low confidence in him. Use the symbol ± for moderate confidence and the symbol + for high confidence. As a final step, explain the bases for the symbols that you selected.

Table 3.3. New York City's Mayor Takes Educators' Advice about Students' Smartphones

Groups	Response*	Explanation
Teachers		
Parents		

*– Low
± Moderate
+ High

Activity 3.4

New York City's mayor later ignored educators' advice about students' smartphones. Asserting that he was in the best position to look after students, he announced that he personally would make decisions about their phones. How did groups respond?

Table 3.4 identifies two New York City groups: teachers and parents.

Complete the table by indicating the ways in which the groups responded to the mayor. You can use symbols.

Use the symbol – if the groups expressed low confidence in him. Use the symbol ± for moderate confidence and the symbol + for high confidence. As a final step, explain the bases for the symbols that you selected.

Table 3.4. New York City's Mayor Ignores Educators' Advice about Students' Smartphones

Groups	Response*	Explanation
Teachers		
Parents		

*– Low
± Moderate
+ High

SUMMARY

T-Mobile executives explained that they were in the best position to look after customers: they therefore placed restrictions on their smartphone plans. A New York City mayor insisted that he was in the best position to look after students: he therefore forbade them from bringing smartphones to school.

Chapter 4

Who Should Take Charge of Assessment?

[States] have embraced value-added testing.
—Mark Schug & Scott Niederjohn, 2009

States have to trust [that] the vendor is designing a [value-added] test system that is fair.
—Council of Chief State School Officers Executive Janice Poda, quoted by Banchero & Kesmodel, 2011

[Test vendors] compute value-added scores in different ways [for clients].
—Stephen Raudenbush & Marshall Jean, 2012

[If they did not use value-added test scores,] Florida and Texas [would] look worse.
—David Leonhardt, 2015

Politicians had doubts about the assessment procedures that fiscal and educational analysts were using. They took charge and prescribed new procedures for both groups.

DYNAMICALLY SCORED BUDGETS

Federal politicians regularly sponsored pricey public projects. However, they worried that they would be challenged by fiscally conservative colleagues.

The sponsoring politicians hired fiscal analysts to help them. They directed them to appraise their projects, highlighting their complex benefits. They distributed the appraisals to their legislative opponents. They also shared them with lobbyists, journalists, and members of the public.

The politicians were pleased with the analysts that they had hired. Nonetheless, they realized that independent fiscal analysts appraised all major federal projects. They were chagrined when these analysts drew very different conclusions.

The politicians admonished the independent analysts. They accused them of employing inappropriate accounting procedures. They explained that they had used procedures that focused solely on the direct benefits of their projects.

The politicians told the analysts that they should use dynamic scoring. They explained that these procedures examined the indirect benefits of massive and complicated projects.

The politicians used defense budgets to illustrate their point. They believed that the analysts had erred when they concentrated on the way that these budgets affected the country's military readiness. They ordered them to go back; use dynamic scoring; and examine the way they affected industrial output, employment rate, and the economy.

The politicians were delighted with dynamically scored defense budgets. They noted that they appeared much more reasonable (Marcos, 2015).

Enthusiasts

Politicians had discovered an ingenious way to make expensive governmental budgets palatable. However, they still needed a way to make massive tax cuts palatable.

Those politicians who recommended tax cuts had personal confidence in them. Nonetheless, they were upset with the many critics who did not share their confidence.

The critics complained that tax cuts deprived the federal government of essential revenue. They persuaded constituents to repeat the complaints.

The politicians felt pressure to demonstrate that tax cuts had benefits. They realized that their critics would rely on the appraisals that independent fiscal analysts made. They were nervous because those analysts employed traditional accounting procedures.

Even the independent fiscal analysts had been able to demonstrate that tax cuts benefitted wealthy individuals and prosperous corporations. However, they had trouble showing that they benefitted the federal government.

The politicians asked the analysts to go back and dynamically score the budgets associated with tax cuts. They were hopeful that the results would surprise critics, skeptical constituents, and even the analysts themselves.

After they switched to dynamic scoring, the fiscal analysts did change their appraisals. By linking the massive tax cuts to accelerated spending, they were able to predict that they would create significant tax revenue (Bartlett, 2013; Krugman, 2015).

Proponents of dynamic scoring believed that the analysts had supplied the logic they needed to justify tax cuts. Although they easily comprehended this logic, they worried whether the public would grasp it.

The proponents looked for a group that could simplify the rationale for dynamically scored budgets. They appealed to journalists. They made a special plea to those at the *Wall Street Journal* and other business-oriented publications (Ip, 2015; Jacobs, 2015).

Skeptics

Some persons were skeptical of dynamic scoring. Congressional Democrats were skeptical when it was applied to tax cuts. They questioned whether Republicans should be using it to justify a huge cut in 2015.

Democrats challenged the Republicans when they asserted that they were enacting a tax cut to increase governmental revenue. They claimed that they genuinely were enacting it to reward wealthy donors and friendly corporations.

The Republicans did not flinch when Democrats slammed their budget. They agreed to send it to the nonpartisan analysts at the federal Office of Management and Budget. They asked them to appraise it objectively. However, they insisted that they use dynamic scoring (Flynn, 2015).

The Democrats believed that the Republicans were using dynamic scoring as a type of budgetary legerdemain. Nonetheless, they did not think that they could stop them on their own. They needed an influential group to assist them. They asked liberal-leaning journalists, such as those at the *New York Times* and the *Washington Post*, to arouse public opposition to the procedure (*New York Times* Editorial Board, 2014, 2015a; *Washington Post* Editorial Board, 2015).

VALUE-ADDED TESTS

Politicians had used dynamic scoring to highlight the indirect fiscal benefits of costly governmental expenditures. Pleased with the results, they later used it to highlight the indirect fiscal benefits of revenue cuts.

Politicians were excited about dynamic scoring. They judged that it was an invaluable tool with which to deal with troubling budgetary issues. They hoped to find a similar tool with which to deal with nettlesome educational issues such as commercial educational testing.

Politicians had for decades depended on educational testing firms for campaign donations. They detected a way to show appreciation: they promised to create a national educational movement that featured their products.

During the administration of George W. Bush, conservative politicians were determined to launch the new test-centered educational movement.

Aided by lobbyists from the testing firms, they persuaded liberal politicians to help them.

The bipartisan group of politicians announced that they would mandate many more commercial educational tests. They stated that they needed these tests to hold students accountable. However, they added that they also needed them to hold instructors accountable (Giordano, 2016).

Enthusiasts

Teachers were surprised by the politicians. They also were disconcerted by their focus on instructors.

The teachers did not doubt that instructors were responsible for their students' test scores. However, they believed that they were only partially responsible. They urged the politicians to reconsider their plan.

The politicians were not intimidated when scrappy teachers confronted them. They threw several jabs at them: they endorsed commercial tests, required schools to use them, and ordered schools to rank instructors on the bases of students' test scores.

The teachers counterpunched: they pointed out that the test scores were influenced by extraneous factors over which instructors had no control. They gave examples of economic, social, and linguistic factors that could influence test scores. They alleged that these factors could invalidate the scores and jeopardize educational initiatives linked to them (David, 2010; Giordano, 2005, 2016).

The politicians had not expected the counterpunches. They staggered unsteadily from them.

The politicians realized that they had underestimated the stamina, strength, and skill of the teachers. They concluded that they would need help if they were going to knock them off their feet.

The politicians went to the executives at commercial testing firms. They recounted the details of their bout with the teachers. They then made two requests. They wanted the executives to identify the extraneous factors that influenced test scores. They also wanted them to come up with a way to compensate for those factors.

The testing executives did not personally assist the politicians. However, they did tell the scholastic analysts on their staffs to help them.

The scholastic analysts ensured that tests were reliable and valid. They administered prototypical versions of tests and then statistically sifted through the results. They were sure that they could use their expertise to help the politicians.

The scholastic analysts described how government fiscal analysts had applied dynamic scoring to budgets. They emphasized how the analysts had identified indirect benefits, assigned values to them, and then used that information to reframe the budgets.

The scholastic analysts wished to adapt dynamic scoring for education. They explained that they could identify the extraneous factors that affected test scores, assign values to them, and use that information to recalculate scores.

Some scholastic analysts referred to their new procedures as value-added modeling; others referred to them as value-added testing. They anticipated that politicians would prefer the latter term, which made the procedures seem a bit less arcane (Dillon, 2010).

The scholastic analysts wanted to make sure that the politicians would be satisfied with value-added testing. They therefore invited them to identify the extraneous factors that affected scores. They explained that this information would be used to statistically adjust original test scores.

The analysts also invited the politicians to indicate the importance that they assigned to each extraneous factor. They explained that this was another type of information with which to adjust test scores.

The politicians were pleased with value-added testing. They were confident that it would help them during subsequent bouts with the teachers. They intended to use it to block the teachers' blows.

The politicians were pleased with value-added testing for another reason: they had devised it by collaborating with for-profit testing firms. They touted this paradigm as the ideal way to solve nettlesome educational problems (Harris, 2015a; *Wall Street Journal* Editorial Board, 2015).

The politicians from certain states, such as Texas and Florida, were pleased with value-added testing for one more reason. They had been guaranteed that this type of testing would make their states rise in national scholastic rankings. They beamed after the prediction turned out to be accurate (Chingos, 2015; Leonhardt, 2015).

Skeptics

Teachers were concerned about value-added testing. They had multiple questions about the technical aspects. They addressed them to the scholastic analysts at commercial testing firms.

The teachers had been assured that the scholastic analysts had identified the extraneous factors affecting students' test scores. They asked them how they had come up with those factors.

The analysts replied that they had not come up with factors on their own. They confessed that they had invited federal politicians to specify them. They also confessed that they had given similar invitations to governors, state legislators, the members of political foundations, and the bureaucrats at state offices of education.

The teachers were displeased. They chastised scholastic analysts for the groups that they had consulted. They also chastised them for the groups that they had failed to consult: instructors, school administrators, parents, and the members of professional educational associations (Raudenbush & Jean, 2012).

The teachers requested still additional technical information about value-added testing. They wanted details about the statistical formula that the scholastic analysts had used to adjust test scores (Dillon, 2010).

The scholastic analysts acknowledged that they did not have a single formula but rather multiple formulas. They had custom-designed formulas for the individual states with which their firms had contracts. In fact, they even had custom-designed them for the school districts with which they had contracts (Giordano, 2016).

The teachers again were displeased. They censured the analysts for deferring to the advice of clients. They explained that they had flagrant conflicts of interests because they depended on those clients for funding (Banchero & Kesmodel, 2011).

EXAMINING QUESTIONS ABOUT CONTROVERSIAL ASSESSMENT

Politicians devised an ingenious way to change the image of government spending: they replaced traditional budgets with dynamically scored budgets. They came up with an equally ingenious way to change the image of scholastic achievement: they replaced traditional testing with value-added testing.

Activity 4.1

Fiscal analysts had for decades used traditional accounting procedures. They ignored the indirect benefits of governmental projects and tax cuts. How did groups respond?

Table 4.1 identifies two groups: politicians and journalists.

Complete the table by indicating the ways in which the groups responded to the fiscal analysts. You can use symbols.

Use the symbol – if the groups expressed low confidence in the analysts. Use the symbol ± for moderate confidence and the symbol + for high confidence. As a final step, explain the bases for the symbols that you selected.

You can rely on the information in this chapter, additional information, or the information cited in the references. If you are reading this chapter with colleagues, you can confer with them.

Who Should Take Charge of Assessment? 43

Table 4.1. Fiscal Analysts Ignore Indirect Benefits of Governmental Initiatives

Groups	Response*	Explanation
Politicians		
Journalists		

*– Low
± Moderate
+ High

Activity 4.2

Fiscal analysts began to use dynamic scoring. They then highlighted the indirect benefits of governmental projects and tax cuts. How did groups respond?

Table 4.2 identifies two groups: politicians and journalists.

Complete the table by indicating the ways in which the groups responded to the fiscal analysts. You can use symbols.

Use the symbol – if the groups expressed low confidence in the analysts. Use the symbol ± for moderate confidence and the symbol + for high confidence. As a final step, explain the bases for the symbols that you selected.

Table 4.2. Fiscal Analysts Highlight Indirect Benefits of Governmental Initiatives

Groups	Response*	Explanation
Politicians		
Journalists		

*– Low
± Moderate
+ High

Activity 4.3

Scholastic analysts had for decades used actual test scores. They ignored extraneous influences affecting the scores. How did groups respond?

Table 4.3 identifies two groups: politicians and teachers.

Complete the table by indicating the ways in which the groups responded to the scholastic analysts. You can use symbols.

Use the symbol − if the groups expressed low confidence in the analysts. Use the symbol ± for moderate confidence and the symbol + for high confidence. As a final step, explain the bases for the symbols that you selected.

Table 4.3. Scholastic Analysts Ignore Extraneous Influences on Test Scores

Groups	Response*	Explanation
Politicians		
Teachers		

*− Low
± Moderate
+ High

Activity 4.4

Scholastic analysts began to calculate "value-added" test scores. They then highlighted extraneous influences affecting the scores. How did groups respond?

Table 4.4 identifies two groups: politicians and teachers.

Complete the table by indicating the ways in which the groups responded to the scholastic analysts. You can use symbols.

Use the symbol − if the groups expressed low confidence in the analysts. Use the symbol ± for moderate confidence and the symbol + for high confidence. As a final step, explain the bases for the symbols that you selected.

Table 4.4. Scholastic Analysts Highlight Extraneous Influences on Test Scores

Groups	Response*	Explanation
Politicians		
Teachers		

*– Low
± Moderate
+ High

SUMMARY

Politicians identified a new way to calculate governmental budgets. However, they had difficulty demonstrating that the calculations were accurate. When they devised a new way to calculate scholastic test scores, they again had difficulty.

Chapter 5

Who Should Take Charge of Grading?

> Does your school hand out too many A's?
> —Katherine Schulten, 2013
>
> I'm losing confidence in what a school grade means.
> —Parent Becki Couch, quoted by Brooks, 2013
>
> [State officials are] concerned that some teachers might be grading too easily.
> —Javier Hernández, 2013
>
> What should you do about [easy grading]?
> —Samantha Lindsay, 2015
>
> C is the new F.
> —John Turner, 2016

Lawyers were frustrated by courtroom videos. Politicians were frustrated by scholastic grading. Both groups took charge and made controversial changes.

CONTROVERSIAL COURTROOM STRATEGIES

Lawyers looked for ways to enhance courtroom arguments. They asked videographers for advice.

The videographers were sure that they could help. They offered to record depositions from witnesses who could not appear in court. They then would display the videos during court sessions. They added that they could manipulate camera angle, lighting, and sound to affect the credibility of these witnesses.

The videographers had still more advice for the defense attorneys. They explained that they could simulate the sequence of events at a crime scene.

These simulations could demonstrate the actual or hypothetical interrelationships among characters, events, and pieces of evidence.

The videographers had confidence in their videos. They guaranteed that they would complement, enhance, and strengthen arguments (Dougherty, 2014; Schwartz, 2009).

The videographers hoped that defense attorneys would take their advice. They were pleased when they experimentally commissioned deposition and simulation videos; they beamed when they continued to commission them for decades (Clifford, 2007; McWilliams, 2009).

Enthusiasts

Defense attorneys commissioned deposition videos and simulation videos for the innocent—guilty phases of trials. They were convinced that they protected their clients' interests (Feigenson & Spiesel, 2009).

When defense attorneys argued criminal cases, they tried to avoid convictions. Needless to say, they sometimes did not succeed. They then had to represent their clients during the penalty phases of trials.

The defense attorneys wished to minimize the sentences that clients would receive. They once again went to the videographers. However, this time they did not ask for their advice. They already had made up their minds about the type of videos they needed.

The defense attorneys needed videos to sway jurors and judges. They wanted ones that highlighted positive experiences and character traits of their convicted clients.

The defense attorneys gave an example of the experiences and traits in which they were interested. They predicted that prior membership in the armed services would be very helpful to clients.

The defense attorneys requested videos that contained images of clients wearing uniforms, testimonials from their military-era colleagues, stock military footage, and patriotic music. They were sure that these videos would elicit empathy from the persons in the courtroom, including the jurors and the judge.

Defense attorneys were excited about character videos. However, they realized that they would be too expensive for many defendants. They therefore recommended them only to their wealthy clients (Clifford, 2015).

Skeptics

Prosecutors sometimes were displeased with the ways that deposition and simulation videos had been filmed and edited. Nonetheless, the videos allowed them to supplement opening statements, provided the basis to challenge courtroom witnesses face-to-face, and even embellished closing arguments (Litigation Technology Services, 2011).

Although the prosecutors did not object to deposition or simulation videos, they objected sternly to character videos. They implored the judges to prohibit them during the penalty phases of trials.

The prosecutors stated that character videos, which were designed to elicit emotional responses, comprised a reckless type of rhetoric. They asked judges to make the defense attorneys rely on oral remarks instead. They reasoned that oral remarks were more likely to elicit logical responses from the courtroom participants.

The defense attorneys were ready with a rejoinder. They highlighted the courtroom rhetorical techniques that they historically had used to arouse sympathy. They contended that these techniques, which were universally accepted, were no different from the character videos (Clifford, 2015).

CONTROVERSIAL EDUCATIONAL STRATEGIES

Persons had been complaining about American schools for decades. Many of them had become fierce critics.

The critics were not satisfied with identifying school problems; they had advice about how to solve them. Although they gave their advice to superintendents and principals, they were disappointed when these groups showed little interest.

The critics wanted to get more attention. They realized that they would get it only if powerful groups took their side. They went to state and federal politicians.

The critics recapitulated the advice that they had given to school administrators. They repeated their recommendations about funding, personnel, curricula, instruction, textbooks, technology, and tests.

The critics were pleased when politicians listened respectfully to them. They were even more pleased when they pledged to incorporate their advice into governmental educational policies.

The critics initially commended the politicians. They thanked them for giving them the chance to get more involved with the schools. They believed that they were about to have an impact on the nation's educational agenda.

The critics later went to the politicians again. They explained that they wanted to do still more for the schools. They wanted to get involved with day-to-day management. For example, they wanted to determine how teachers assigned grades to students (Giordano, 2012a, 2012b).

Politicians historically had directed local school administrators to handle grading. They expected them to develop policies; make sure that they were fair; and arbitrate the disagreements that inevitably arose among educators, students, and parents.

The school administrators had been pleased with the politicians' laissez-faire attitudes toward grades. They had developed grading policies on their own. They made sure that they were sensitive to the instruction, curricula, textbooks, and classroom activities within their districts (Giordano, 2004, 2009, 2014).

Because they were customizing grading policies for the districts in which they were employed, the school administrators consulted with the local teachers, parents, and community members. They continually asked whether they supported their policies. They made changes when they did not.

The school administrators also asked politicians how they felt about their grading policies. They had been pleased when they replied that they were satisfied. They noted that they had given this reply for decades. However, they later detected a change in their attitudes.

The politicians eventually became less cheerful about grading. In fact, they began to complain loudly. They repeated the complaints that they had heard from the school critics. They contended that that grading policies had become too lax. They explained that students were receiving indefensibly high grades.

The politicians scolded the school administrators for shoddy grading policies. The administrators were accused of deliberately mismanaging the grades in order to make weak students appear strong (Giordano, 2012b).

The politicians were fed up with the school administrators. They stated that they were relieving them of their grading duties. They announced that they personally would take charge.

Enthusiasts

State politicians were excited that they had the chance to design grading policies. However, none of them was more enthusiastic than Jeb Bush.

Jeb Bush aspired to become the governor of Florida. Although he attracted significant funding for a campaign in 1994, he did not succeed.

Bush concluded that he had lost the election because he failed to focus on an issue that energized voters. He resolved to not make this error again: he would find a stimulating issue for the next election.

Jeb Bush did not attract much attention when he identified education as the hot issue on which he would focus his new campaign. However, he aroused curiosity when he explained that he was primarily concerned about grading practices.

Jeb Bush decried the grading practices that were common in Florida's schools. He alleged that they did not provide meaningful information about children's academic progress.

Jeb Bush believed that many persons shared his dismal view of grading. He was convinced that school critics, businesspeople, fellow politicians, and some parents shared it. He promised them that he would make revolutionary changes.

Jeb Bush won the 1999 election. However, he waited until he had assumed office to reveal his revolutionary grading policy. The policy had three steps: all school administrators had to purchase the same tests, compute scores on them in the same fashion, and then follow the same procedure to transform the scores into letter grades.

Jeb Bush was certain that state legislators and businesspeople would approve of his grading policy. Nonetheless, he was not sure how parents would react to it. He anticipated that some would object. He anticipated that even some of those who supported the policy would change their minds about it if their children's grades began to plummet (Giordano, 2016).

Jeb Bush did not wish to antagonize the parents. He looked for a way to appease them. He told them that he was not truly interested in assigning grades to their children. He stated that he was interested in assigning grades to schools.

Jeb Bush explained why he wished to grade the schools. He intended to get rid of the administrators and teachers who worked at schools with low grades. He stated that these personnel changes would eventually benefit students.

George W. Bush admired the grading reforms that his brother Jeb had initiated in Florida. After he became president, he persuaded a bipartisan group of federal legislators to make similar reforms. They codified them in the No Child Left Behind Law of 2002.

Barack Obama was impressed by the steps that the Bush brothers had taken to make grading more rigorous. He particularly admired the way that they had diverted attention from students to schools. He resolved to follow their example.

After he became president, Obama instructed his secretary of education to grade every school in the nation. He directed the secretary to display the results on a parent-accessible website.

Skeptics

Educators realized that they had lost control of grading. They were disconcerted. Unionized educators were especially disconcerted.

The unionized educators had been extremely partisan: they had refused to make financial contributions to politicians who did not sympathize with them. They realized that these politicians, who already were hostile toward them, would use grading reforms to retaliate. They became even more worried when the hostile politicians recruited a broad range of legislative allies (Brenneman, 2015; Garrow, 2013; Ujifusa, 2015).

The reform-minded legislators were impressed by Jeb Bush's early efforts to change the way that grades were assigned in Florida. They copied him: they prescribed tests, procedures for computing scores on them, and guidelines for transforming the scores into grades.

The legislators also were impressed by Bush's practice of relying on grades to reward schools and teachers. They stated that they would use enhanced operating budgets to reward the schools. They added that they would use bonuses, salary increases, and job security to reward the teachers.

The teachers objected. They noted that new grading policies assumed that instructors and their schools were the primary influences on scholastic achievement. They identified many additional factors that were extremely influential.

The teachers predicted that instructors would suffer because of the new grading policies. They later documented that those who taught students with disabilities were penalized. They explained that these instructors were not responsible for their students' test-linked grades.

The teachers also predicted that schools would suffer because of the new grading policies. They later documented problems for those that served migrant families, households in which limited English was spoken, high-crime neighborhoods, and economically depressed communities. They explained that these schools were only partially responsible for students' test results and the grades that were linked to them (Giordano, 2004, 2012b, 2016).

Many parents sided with the teachers. They joined those who were protesting government-developed grading policies. They were convinced that these policies were damaging schools, teachers, and students (Sanchez, 2015; Taylor & Rich, 2015).

EXAMINING CONTROVERSIAL STRATEGIES

Defense attorneys contended that a novel type of video promoted courtroom justice. Politicians contended that a novel type of grading promoted student achievement. However, both groups struggled to deal with skeptics.

Activity 5.1

Defense attorneys relied on technical experts to design courtroom videos. They noted that their videos deposed witnesses and demonstrated sequences of events at crime scenes. How did groups respond?

Table 5.1 identifies two groups: clients and prosecutors.

Complete the table by indicating the ways in which the groups responded to the attorneys. You can use symbols.

Use the symbol – if the groups expressed low confidence in them. Use the symbol ± for moderate confidence and the symbol + for high confidence. As a final step, explain the bases for the symbols that you selected.

You can rely on the information in this chapter, additional information, or the information cited in the references. If you are reading this chapter with colleagues, you can confer with them.

Table 5.1. Attorneys Rely on Technical Experts to Design Courtroom Videos

Groups	Response*	Explanation
Clients		
Prosecutors		

* – Low
± Moderate
+ High

Activity 5.2

Defense attorneys began to personally design courtroom videos. They made sure that they highlighted the positive character traits and experiences of their clients. How did groups respond?

Table 5.2 identifies two groups: clients and prosecutors.

Complete the table by indicating the ways in which the groups responded to the attorneys. You can use symbols.

Use the symbol – if the groups expressed low confidence in them. Use the symbol ± for moderate confidence and the symbol + for high confidence. As a final step, explain the bases for the symbols that you selected.

Table 5.2. Attorneys Personally Design Courtroom Videos

Groups	Response*	Explanation
Clients		
Prosecutors		

* – Low
± Moderate
+ High

Activity 5.3

Politicians relied on school administrators to develop grading policies. They noted that their policies were sensitive to the concerns of local constituents. How did groups respond?

Table 5.3 identifies two groups: teachers and parents.

Complete the table by indicating the ways in which the groups responded to the politicians. You can use symbols.

Use the symbol– if the groups expressed low confidence in them. Use the symbol ± for moderate confidence and the symbol + for high confidence. As a final step, explain the bases for the symbols that you selected.

Table 5.3. Politicians Rely on School Administrators to Develop Grading Policies

Groups	Response*	Explanation
Teachers		
Parents		

*– Low
± Moderate
+ High

Activity 5.4

Politicians began to personally develop grading policies. They made sure that they were sensitive to the concerns of school critics. How did groups respond?

Table 5.4 identifies two groups: teachers and parents.

Complete the table by indicating the ways in which the groups responded to the politicians. You can use symbols.

Use the symbol – if the groups expressed low confidence in them. Use the symbol ± for moderate confidence and the symbol + for high confidence. As a final step, explain the bases for the symbols that you selected.

Table 5.4. Politicians Personally Develop Grading Policies

Groups	Response*	Explanation
Teachers		
Parents		

* – Low
± Moderate
+ High

SUMMARY

Lawyers contended that a novel type of video promoted courtroom justice. Politicians contended that a novel type of grading helped student achievement. However, both groups had difficulty convincing skeptics.

Chapter 6

Who Should Take Charge of Truants?

[If you only send some truants to criminal court], what are you gonna' do with the rest of 'em?
—Texas Justice of the Peace Lanny Moriarty, quoted in "Texas Honor Student," 2012

Only two states . . . send truants to adult criminal court.
—"Texas Decriminalizing Students' Truancy," 2015

Texas . . . has sent about 100,000 students a year to criminal court . . . for missing school.
—"Texas Law," 2015

Close to 100 percent of [Texas's truancy] cases are caused by social and economic conditions.
—Texas State Senator John Whitmire, quoted by Feldman, 2015

A mayor disapproved of the nontraditional artists who performed on pedestrian plazas in his city: he took charge and pledged to tear up the plazas. State legislators disapproved of truant students: they took charge and pledged to prosecute them. Both groups were surprised by the citizen activists whom they aroused.

AN IRATE MAYOR

New York City's Times Square is frequented by fifty thousand persons a day. It has been colorfully called the "Crossroads of the World" (Goodson, 2011).

Persons had varied reasons for going to Times Square. Some went because they were inspired by the references to the area in literature, music, theater, and cinema. Others went for dining and entertainment.

For generations, visitors had been struck by the distinctiveness of Times Square. When they went to the city's other outdoor sites, they found plazas where they could relax, read a newspaper, sip a drink, or meet with friends. When they went to Times Square, they found pedestrian-jammed sidewalks and vehicle-clogged streets.

While serving as New York City's mayor, Michael Bloomberg took note of the throngs that Times Square accommodated. However, he did not think that they were being accommodated properly. He wished to make some changes to the area.

Bloomberg met with Times Square business owners. He also met with local, state, and federal politicians. He asked them to suggest improvements to the neighborhood. However, he cautioned that their suggestions would have to be affordable.

Critics derided Bloomberg's meetings as populist grandstanding. They predicted that they would not lead to affordable changes.

Bloomberg surprised his critics. He was able to come up with a plan that was affordable. He made it affordable by eliciting financial concessions from city agencies, the state, and the federal government. He even extracted concessions from local businesses and the city's utility corporation.

Bloomberg stunned his critics when he presented a plan that was affordable. He stunned them again when he made sure that it represented a shared vision. He attracted support for a proposal to create pedestrian-friendly plazas. He romantically referred to these areas as "urban piazzas" ("Times Square Transformation," 2015).

Bloomberg commenced work on the Times Square renovation during the last year of his political tenure. Although he could not complete it, he took efforts to ensure that it would be finished during his successor's term.

Bill De Blasio succeeded Bloomberg as mayor in 2014. He surprised everyone with his reaction to the new pedestrian plazas: he did not like them.

De Blasio may have disapproved of the pedestrian plazas because of the publicity that they were bringing to his predecessor. If he did, he concealed his feelings. He stated that he was upset about them for a different reason: the unseemly performance artists that they attracted (Kimmelman, 2015).

De Blasio noted that some artists were women without tops. He concluded that they had removed their tops solely to get tips from the crowds.

The mayor directed the police to patrol the plazas, harass the female artists, and force them to cover their breasts. However, he was disappointed when the officers had little impact on the artists.

The mayor came up with a bolder plan. He announced that he was going to tear up the pedestrian plazas on which the women performed; he explained that he was going to convert them back into high-traffic streets.

Enthusiasts

De Blasio realized that his proposal was controversial. He knew that residents and visitors, even though they had been inconvenienced by years of construction, were pleased with the plazas. He expected them to resist his proposal.

De Blasio also expected political and business leaders to resist his proposal. After all, they had contributed over $30 million to construct the plazas.

De Blasio even expected journalists to resist his proposal. Although some of them had initially been ambivalent about the renovation, they eventually became excited about the results.

De Blasio braced for opposition to his proposal. Nonetheless, he still expected significant support. He assumed that many New Yorkers shared his distaste for topless street performers. He hoped that they would become his allies (Whitford, 2015).

The mayor also expected support from cab drivers, emergency vehicle operators, automobile drivers, and delivery truck drivers. He supposed that they were annoyed because the pedestrian plazas had slowed the flow of traffic in midtown Manhattan. He assumed that they would want him to tear up the plazas (Dawsey & Gay, 2015; Grynbaum & Flegenheimer, 2015).

Skeptics

Business owners had collaborated with Bloomberg to design the Times Square project. They then had partially funded it. Even though they had to tolerate the disruption from demolition and construction, they had never lost confidence in the project.

The business owners had remained optimistic because they predicted that the project eventually would draw larger-than-ever crowds to the area. They were gratified when their prediction turned out to be correct ("Bloomberg Unveils Redesign," 2013).

When the business owners learned of De Blasio's plan, they were shocked. They were convinced that it was wrong-headed and reactionary. Nonetheless, they were not sure that they were strong enough to stop it. They asked journalists to highlight their concerns and stir up citizen activists.

The journalists were intrigued that their mayor intended to demolish such a high-profile, expensive, and protracted building project. They were even more intrigued after he explained his reasoning.

The mayor explained to the journalists that he did not disapprove of the plazas themselves, the residents who relaxed on them, or the tourists who passed through them. He disapproved only of the topless artists who performed on them.

Journalists had been skeptical when De Blasio's predecessor had presented a plan to renovate Times Square. They had worried that the project would be too expensive to be completed. However, they became more and more pleased as the project progressed. They eventually could not deny its multiple benefits.

The journalists wondered why their current mayor did not see the benefits of the plazas. They also wondered why he was so upset about the artists on them. They reminded him that the city did not prohibit street artists from performing, panhandling, or even going topless (McGeehan & Grynbaum, 2015).

Most local residents were as confused as the journalists. They did not understand why their mayor was focusing so intently on the Times Square artists. They believed that he was creating problems far greater than those that he was trying to solve. They became citizen activists: they demanded that he leave the city's artists and plazas alone (Budin, 2015).

IRATE LEGISLATORS

State legislators were upset about children who were absent from school. They were especially upset about those who were routinely absent. They knew that they were not learning. They suspected that they were not behaving.

Historically, the state legislators had a common sense way of responding to truant students: they delegated responsibility to local schoolboards. They counted on the boards to establish policies and procedures to get the students back into their classrooms. They assumed that the schoolboards would consult with parents about the best way to handle truancy.

Parents were generally pleased with the manner in which schoolboards handled truancy. When they were dealing with the members of elected boards, they made it clear that they should follow their advice if they wished to be reelected. They were gratified when they listened to them and treated truancy as a scholastic problem. They showed their gratitude by reelecting them.

Parents were equally blunt when they were dealing with members of mayor-appointed schoolboards. They warned them to listen to their advice if they wanted their mayors to be reelected. They repeated this warning to the mayors as well.

Although parents approved of manner in which schoolboards were handling truant students, many state legislators did not. The legislators believed that the boards were being far too lenient. They had a solution for this problem: they would replace the schoolboards' local policies with their own statewide policies.

The disgruntled legislators looked for truancy policies that had been adopted in other states. They searched for those that were more rigorous than their own and that could easily be expropriated. Many of them were impressed by the policies in Texas.

The Texas legislators had required that school administrators alert the police when students exhibited routine absences. They even defined routine absences: four unexcused missed classes during a four-week-long period or ten missed classes during a six-month-long period. They directed the police to locate the truants and make sure that they appeared in adult courtrooms ("Texas Law," 2015).

Texas legislators believed that judges who ran courtrooms for adult criminals were in the best position to deal with truants. They required them to discipline students as young as twelve years old.

Texas legislators were pleased after they enacted their statewide truancy policy. They smiled with satisfaction as the criminal judges began to discipline hundreds of students. They beamed when they eventually were disciplining tens of thousands each year.

The legislators even told the judges how to handle truant students. They encouraged them to fine the truant students. Anticipating that they would be unable to collect the fines from the students, they directed them to make their parents responsible for them.

Enthusiasts

Legislators in several states admired the Texas truancy law. They also admired the zeal with which it was enforced it. They noted that the Texans eventually were accounting for more than half of the nation's truancy prosecutions.

Wyoming's legislators copied the Texans: they sent their own truant students to adult criminal courtrooms. However, Louisiana's legislators decided to be a bit less stringent: they sent them to juvenile courtrooms or family courtrooms.

Legislators in several states came up with additional ways to punish truant students and their parents. For example, those in Louisiana took driving licenses away from the students and then jailed their parents. Those in Tennessee reduced any welfare payments that the parents were receiving (LA Rev Stat § 17:233, 2015; Thompson, 2014).

Some hard-nosed city officials disapproved of the way that their state legislators were handling truant students. Distressed that they were not arresting the parents of these students, they began to arrest them on their own.

The city officials in one Pennsylvania community hoped to create a national stir by jailing the parents of children whose truancies had resulted in unpaid fines or court costs. However, they caused the wrong type of stir after they arrested one parent, placed her in a cell, and then allowed her to die there unattended (Goldstein, 2015; Popovich, 2014).

Skeptics

State legislators were sure that strict truancy policies benefitted children. However, they failed to convince some of their constituents. They had an especially hard time convincing teachers.

Teachers noted that many students were truant because of extenuating circumstances. They ticked off a list of circumstances that included homelessness, pregnancy, and employment. They argued that these students should not be treated as criminals ("Texas Honor Student," 2012; Wilkie, 2015).

The teachers highlighted the connection between psychological disabilities and truancy. They pointed out that students with these disabilities had been taken to court without even notifying their school-based psychologists. They decried the damage that they had suffered (Feldman, 2015).

Many parents were skeptical of legislator-developed truancy policies. They shared the concerns that the teachers had expressed. However, they had an additional reason for being skeptical.

The parents questioned whether authorities were enforcing legislator-developed truancy policies in an equitable fashion. They noted that they were disciplining a disproportionately high number of students from racial, ethnic, and economic minority groups (Dominus, 2016; Popovich, 2014).

Many of the parents in Texas became citizen activists: they asked their legislators to go back and reevaluate the truancy policies that they had developed. Although they conceded that they may have helped some students, they contended that they had harmed many more. They were joined by citizen activists in other states, who demanded that their legislators return the authority for truancy to school boards ("Texas Law," 2015).

EXAMINING QUESTIONS FROM CITIZEN ACTIVISTS

A mayor pledged to tear up pedestrian plazas in his city; he explained that he was trying to force out the artists who performed on them. He was surprised when citizen activists challenged him.

State legislators pledged to prosecute truant students: they explained that they were trying to force them back to school. They were surprised when citizen activists challenged them.

Activity 6.1

Mayor Bloomberg was concerned about New York City's residents and visitors. He backed a local coalition's plan to construct pedestrian-friendly plazas for them. How did groups respond?

Who Should Take Charge of Truants? 63

Table 6.1 identifies two groups: journalists and the public.

Complete the table by indicating the ways in which the groups responded to the mayor. You can use symbols.

Use the symbol – if the groups expressed low confidence in him. Use the symbol ± for moderate confidence and the symbol + for high confidence. As a final step, explain the bases for the symbols that you selected.

You can rely on the information in this chapter, additional information, or the information cited in the references. If you are reading this chapter with colleagues, you can confer with them.

Table 6.1. A New York City Mayor Endorses a Local Plan for Pedestrian-Friendly Plazas

Groups	Response*	Explanation
Journalists		
Public		

*– Low
± Moderate
+ High

Activity 6.2

Mayor De Blasio disapproved of the nontraditional artists who were performing on the city's pedestrian-friendly plazas. He personally came up with a plan to get rid of them: he would tear up the plazas. How did groups respond?

Table 6.2 identifies two groups: journalists and the public.

Complete the table by indicating the ways in which the groups responded to the mayor. You can use symbols.

Use the symbol – if the groups expressed low confidence in him. Use the symbol ± for moderate confidence and the symbol + for high confidence. As a final step, explain the bases for the symbols that you selected.

Table 6.2. A New York City Mayor Devises His Own Plan for Pedestrian-Friendly Plazas

Groups	Response*	Explanation
Journalists		
Public		

*– Low
± Moderate
+ High

Activity 6.3

State legislators were concerned about truant students. They initially backed local schoolboards' plans for dealing with them.

Table 6.3 identifies two groups: teachers and parents.

Complete the table by indicating the ways in which the groups responded to the legislators. You can use symbols.

Use the symbol – if the groups expressed low confidence in them. Use the symbol ± for moderate confidence and the symbol + for high confidence. As a final step, explain the bases for the symbols that you selected.

Table 6.3. Legislators Endorse Local Plans for Truant Students

Groups	Response*	Explanation
Teachers		
Parents		

*– Low
± Moderate
+ High

Activity 6.4

State legislators disapproved of the manner in which local schoolboards were handling truant students. They personally came up with a plan to get them back in school: they would send them to criminal courts.

Table 6.4 identifies two groups: teachers and parents.

Complete the table by indicating the ways in which the groups responded to the legislators. You can use symbols.

Use the symbol – if the groups expressed low confidence in them. Use the symbol ± for moderate confidence and the symbol + for high confidence. As a final step, explain the bases for the symbols that you selected.

Table 6.4. Legislators Devise Their Own Plans for Truant Students

Groups	Response*	Explanation
Teachers		
Parents		

*– Low
± Moderate
+ High

SUMMARY

A mayor wanted to drive the nontraditional artists from his city: he pledged to tear up the pedestrian plazas on which they performed. State legislators wanted to drive truant students back to school: they pledged to prosecute them. They insisted that drastic steps were needed to solve profound problems.

Chapter 7

Who Should Take Charge of Training Principals?

[The Chicago Schools CEO awarded training] contracts to a former employer.
—Mary Ahern, 2015

[The Chicago Schools CEO] was to receive a 10 percent [kickback for the training] contracts.
—Laura Moser, 2015

[The Chicago Schools CEO] pleaded guilty to federal [bribery] charges.
—Troy LaRaviere, 2015

[Critics allege that the indicted training firm] did nothing for the Chicago public schools . . . and that's simply inaccurate.
—Attorney Shelly Kulwin, quoted by Bellware, 2015

When businesspeople took charge of programs to train artists, they used unconventional recruitment practices. When they took charge of programs to train school administrators, they again resorted to unconventional practices.

BUSINESSPEOPLE TRAIN ARTISTS

Many persons aspired to careers in art. They hoped that they would have opportunities to enroll in the professional training programs at universities, art leagues, or art institutes.

The faculty at the traditional training programs required applicants to submit portfolios of their creative works. They then rigorously critiqued them when they were making decisions about those applicants whom they would accept.

Enthusiasts

Applicants were elated when they were admitted into the traditional training programs. They were disappointed when they were rejected.

Businesspeople had good news for the rejected applicants: they were establishing alternative, nontraditional training programs for them. They explained that they only would have to submit a single sketch to their program. They added that they then would have very high chances of being accepted.

The businesspeople believed that they could attract aspiring artists to programs with low admission standards. They believed that they could attract investors if they ran those programs as for-profit ventures (Efland, 1990).

Once they had established their programs, businesspeople had to take several additional steps. They had to make students aware of the programs, persuade them to enroll, and, finally, provide them with training. They immediately realized that they could not replicate the steps that the traditional training programs employed.

The traditional programs had distinguished artists on their staffs. These artists marketed the programs, attracted applicants to them, and instructed the students who were admitted into them.

The businesspeople, who did not have famous artists on their staffs, had to find a distinct way to manage and organize programs. They even had to find a distinct way to publicize them.

The businesspeople turned to trendy ads to advertise their programs. They were pleased when these ads caught the attention of persons who dreamed of becoming artists. However, they needed to ensure that these persons actually applied to the programs.

The businesspeople anticipated that potential students would be paying close attention to tuition. They wrestled with the amount they should charge. They judged that it had to be cheaper than that at the traditional programs. However, they also realized that it had to be substantial enough to make a profit. Most of them settled on several thousand dollars as the price for a complete program (Art Instruction Schools, 2015).

The businesspeople tried to convince prospective students that their tuition was reasonable. They told them that it covered not only the cost of their instruction but also the cost of textual materials and even art supplies (Art Instruction Schools, 2015).

The businesspeople had an additional strategy to convince applicants that their tuition was reasonable. They reminded them of the talent tests that they had to complete to enter their programs. They promised that those applicants with high test scores would receive scholarships for a portion of their tuition.

The businesspeople had to ensure that persons discovered their training programs, applied to them, and actually enrolled in them. However, they then had to provide instruction.

The businesspeople had to make a decision about the instructional approach on which they would rely. They already had one in mind: they would mail out self-instructional booklets.

The businesspeople sent out booklets filled with projects. They also sent out art supplies. They directed students to follow the directions for the assignments in their booklets, use the supplies to complete the assignments, and then return the assignments for grading and feedback.

The students received a booklet and supplies each time they made a tuition payment. After they had finished all of these booklets, they received a certificate of completion.

Skeptics

Some students who enrolled in the alternative artist training programs were satisfied. However, others were not. The disgruntled students complained that the instruction was mediocre, the projects simplistic, the supplies substandard, the feedback inane, and the graduation certificates valueless.

The disgruntled students were displeased with the test that had been used to assess their talent. They fumed after they learned that it had classified every applicant as artistically talented. They also were displeased with the scholarships, which they learned had been awarded to every applicant. They realized that the talent test and the scholarships had been marketing scams (Meier, 2002).

The disgruntled students posted blistering online reviews. They may have hoped to get the attention of managers and investors. However, they primarily hoped to get the attention of aspiring artists ("Complaint Review," 2012; Heller, 2008; Wet Canvas, 2016).

Former students were not the only ones who wished to warn aspiring artists. The faculty members at universities, art institutes, and art leagues gave them cautionary advice. They counseled them to avoid any programs that did not offer opportunities to practice in studios, interact with famous instructors, and collaborate with talented peers (Art Students League, 2016; Eisner, 2002; Wolff & Geahigan, 1997).

Enthusiasts Respond to Skeptics

The businesspeople relied on advertisements to lure persons to their alternative training programs. They placed ads in newspapers, magazines, and comic books. They even placed them on matchbook covers and product labels.

In one particularly famous ad, the businesspeople featured a simple cartoon figure. They put a caption beneath it, challenging persons to "draw me" (Meier, 2002).

The businesspeople at the "draw me" art program encouraged aspiring artists to reproduce the cartoon, submit their sketches to them, discover whether they had talent, and compete for scholarships. They assured them that this entire process was free.

The businesspeople initially could not be sure whether their "draw me" advertising campaign would be effective. They were delighted when it created a deluge of responses. They realized that their income and profits were about to soar.

The businesspeople were wildly successful. Nonetheless, they worried that the success was fleeting. They were disconcerted by the many critics who were attacking them. They noted the fiercest critics were former students.

The businesspeople were faulted for the way they had lured participants to their training programs. They replied that they had employed innovative recruitment strategies. They even conceded that some persons might view their strategies as questionable.

The businesspeople also were faulted for their instruction. They replied that their instruction was atypical. However, they insisted that it still was first-rate.

The businesspeople looked for former students to attest to the quality of instruction. They located some who said that they had enjoyed the instruction. They found others who said that they had learned enough to secure jobs as professional cartoonists and artists (Art Instruction Schools, 2015).

BUSINESSPEOPLE TRAIN SCHOOL ADMINISTRATORS

Rahm Emmanuel had served as President Obama's chief of staff. He resigned that position to run for another office: he wanted to be Chicago's mayor.

Emmanuel organized a well-funded and effective campaign. He then easily won the election.

When he had been in Washington, Emmanuel had attracted attention because of the hard-nosed manner in which he dealt with his staff members. After he moved to Chicago, he attracted attention because of the manner in which he handled unionized teachers.

Emmanuel was stern with the teachers. He chastised them for contributing to the city's educational problems. He claimed them that they were more concerned about their own salaries than the students.

Emmanuel was ready to mete out more than harsh rhetoric to the teachers. He warned them that he personally would decide the conditions under which they earned raises and retained their jobs (Giordano, 2014).

Emmanuel realized that he needed a like-minded school's CEO to help him bridle teachers. He would have preferred a businessperson. However, he worried that a businessperson would be unable to win support from the community's parents and journalists.

Emmanuel had to compromise on the school's CEO: he would have to choose a professional educator. Nonetheless, he was not going to cave in completely: he would make sure that this person had extensive experience with the business community.

Emmanuel hired Barbara Byrd-Bennett. He knew that she had been a teacher, a principal, and an executive-level school administrator. He also was aware that she had worked for a firm that sold textbooks and another that provided for-profit training to school administrators.

Emmanuel wished to avoid controversy when he introduced Byrd-Bennett to the Chicago community. He therefore referred solely to her public school experiences (Chicago Public Schools, 2012).

Enthusiasts

Byrd-Bennett had occupied an executive position in Detroit's public schools. However, she simultaneously held a position with a large textbook firm.

The directors of the textbook firm had hoped that Byrd-Bennett could use her influence in the Detroit schools to benefit them. They were ebullient when she secured a lucrative contract for them ("FBI Looked," 2015; FitzPatrick & Mihalopoulos, 2015).

When she interviewed for the position with the Chicago schools, Byrd-Bennett did not conceal her private-sector experience. She admitted that she had worked for a company that sold textbooks to schools and another that provided for-profit training to them. However, she made it clear that she had severed all connections with these firms.

After she had assumed her new position, Byrd-Bennett announced that she would be making arrangements to train Chicago's principals. She attracted little notice with this announcement. In fact, she attracted hardly any notice even after she announced that the training would cost millions of dollars.

Although Byrd-Bennett did not attract attention with her initial announcements about the training contract, she did attract it with a later announcement. She stated that she would not be accepting bids for the multimillion-dollar contract. She explained that she already had made the decision to hire a private-sector training firm—the firm at which she once had been employed.

Chicagoans had listened to Byrd-Bennett who maintained that she had no conflicting interests with former employers. However, they began to have doubts.

The city's journalists were extremely suspicious of Byrd-Bennett because of the way in which she had arranged the training. They noted that she had not given the local universities a chance to compete for it. They, as well as the faculty at those universities, wondered whether she had an ulterior motive (Schutz, 2015; Silets, 2015).

Byrd-Bennett was ready to answer when critics asked her to explain the manner in which she had awarded the contract. She replied that she had offered it to a private-sector firm because it provided training that was cheaper, more streamlined, and more effective than the training from universities (Silets, 2015; SUPES Academy, 2015).

Byrd-Bennett stated that she had one more reason for arranging the contract in the manner that she had. She explained that both she and the mayor valued collaboration between the private and public sectors (SUPES Academy, 2015).

Skeptics

The local politicians had repeatedly blamed Chicago's principals for the city's educational problems. They believed that they lacked appropriate training. They were gratified when the school's CEO made arrangements for them to participate in additional training.

Some participants were satisfied with the training that their school's CEO arranged. They judged that it was simple, streamlined, and geared to their busy workday schedules.

Other participants were not satisfied with the training. They questioned whether it had been delivered by qualified instructors.

The professors at local universities agreed with the disgruntled program participants: they were skeptical of the instructors. They questioned their qualifications.

The professors maintained that they could have provided better training. They were furious that they had not been given a chance (Schutz, 2015; Silets, 2015).

The professors joined public school teachers, parents, and journalists. The members of this alliance made a joint plea to federal investigators. They urged them to examine the circumstances under which a private firm had obtained a no-bid, multimillion-dollar training contract (Hope, 2015).

Enthusiasts Respond to Skeptics

Federal investigators did examine the principal training contract. They focused their attention on the owners of the firm that had received this contract. They asked them how they had obtained it.

The owners provided a startling revelation. They confessed that they had given Byrd-Bennett a kickback to secure the contract.

The owners stated that they were contrite about the kickback. However, they were not contrite about the training. They insisted that it had been extremely professional. They contended that it had helped the principals as well as the teachers and students for whom they were responsible (Bellware, 2015).

The federal investigators were not impressed by the firm's owners. They recommended criminal indictments for them and for Byrd-Bennett.

Journalists had been distrustful of Byrd-Bennett for some time. They therefore were not that surprised when investigators confirmed that she had demanded money for training contracts. Nonetheless, they were quite surprised when the amount paid to Byrd-Bennett was disclosed: 10 percent of all funds.

Byrd-Bennett later admitted that she was guilty. However, she carefully qualified her plea. She explained that she was guilty of only taking a kickback for the training. She staunchly defended the training itself (Bosman, 2015; "Illinois: Ex-Chicago Schools," 2015).

The journalists were eager to question Byrd-Bennet. However, they also were eager to question Mayor Emmanuel.

The journalists had particularly tough questions for the mayor. They reminded him that he had appointed Byrd-Bennett because of her connection to the business community. They asked whether this connection had contributed to her downfall (Madhani, 2015; Meisner & Perez, 2015).

The mayor refused to comment on Byrd-Bennett, the training firm, or the interactions between them. He explained that he had not been involved. However, he did comment on the training: he characterized it as a boon to school administrators, teachers, and students (Perez, 2015).

EXAMINING EXCULPATORY RESPONSES TO CRITICAL QUESTIONS

Businesspeople established alternative, nontraditional programs to train artists and principals. They admitted that they used questionable practices to recruit students and acquire contracts. Nonetheless, they insisted that they still provided effective training.

Activity 7.1

Businesspeople established alternative programs to train artists. They contended that they were reasonably priced, streamlined, and just as effective as traditional programs. How did groups respond?

Table 7.1 identifies two groups: the students in the alternative training programs and the faculty at traditional training programs.

Complete the table by indicating the ways in which the groups responded to the businesspeople. You can use symbols.

Use the symbol – if the groups expressed low confidence in them. Use the symbol ± for moderate confidence and the symbol + for high confidence. As a final step, explain the bases for the symbols that you selected.

You can rely on the information in this chapter, additional information, or the information cited in the references. If you are reading this chapter with colleagues, you can confer with them.

Table 7.1. Businesspeople Provide Alternative Training for Artists

Groups	Response*	Explanation
Students—Alternative Programs		
Faculty—Traditional Programs		

*– Low
± Moderate
+ High

Activity 7.2

Businesspeople were accused of using devious practices to lure students to alternative training programs. Although they admitted their guilt, they insisted that they still had provided high-quality training. How did groups respond?

Table 7.2 identifies two groups: the students in the alternative training programs and the faculty at traditional training programs.

Complete the table by indicating the ways in which the groups responded to the businesspeople. You can use symbols.

Use the symbol – if the groups expressed low confidence in them. Use the symbol ± for moderate confidence and the symbol + for high confidence. As a final step, explain the bases for the symbols that you selected.

Table 7.2. Businesspeople Defend Their Alternative Training for Artists

Groups	Response*	Explanation
Students—Alternative Programs		
Faculty—Traditional Programs		

*– Low
± Moderate
+ High

Activity 7.3

Businesspeople established an alternative program to train principals for the Chicago schools. They contended that the training was reasonably priced, streamlined, and just as effective as that from the traditional, university-based programs. How did groups respond?

Table 7.3 identifies two Chicago groups: the students in the alternative training program and the faculty at traditional, university-based training programs.

Complete the table by indicating the ways in which the groups responded to the businesspeople. You can use symbols.

Use the symbol – if the groups expressed low confidence in them. Use the symbol ± for moderate confidence and the symbol + for high confidence. As a final step, explain the bases for the symbols that you selected.

Table 7.3. Businesspeople Provide Alternative Training for Chicago's Principals

Groups	Response*	Explanation
Students—Alternative Programs		
Faculty—Traditional Programs		

*– Low
± Moderate
+ High

Activity 7.4

Businesspeople were accused of using devious practices to acquire the Chicago training contract. Although they admitted their guilt, they insisted that they still had provided high-quality training. How did groups respond?

Table 7.4 identifies two Chicago groups: the students in the alternative training program and the faculty at traditional, university-based training programs.

Complete the table by indicating the ways in which the groups responded to the businesspeople. You can use symbols.

Use the symbol – if the groups expressed low confidence in them. Use the symbol ± for moderate confidence and the symbol + for high confidence. As a final step, explain the bases for the symbols that you selected.

Table 7.4. Businesspeople Defend Their Alternative Training for Chicago's Principals

Groups	Response*	Explanation
Students—Alternative Program		
Faculty—Traditional Programs		

*– Low
± Moderate
⁺ High

SUMMARY

Businesspeople established alternative programs to train artists and principals. Even though they admitted that they used devious practices to recruit clients and acquire contracts, they maintained that they still provided effective training.

Chapter 8

Who Should Take Charge of School Technology?

> [The school district] began a rollout of iPads.
> —Meghan Murphy, 2014

> [The iPad rollout] was suspended . . . [after] the cost . . . reached $1.3 billion.
> —Peter Jacobs, 2014

> 67 percent of students . . . said they are more interested in school since they received . . . iPads.
> —Matthew Stolle, 2015

> Every kid should have an iPad [provided by his or her school].
> —New Jersey Governor Chris Christie, quoted by Neff, 2015

Law school administrators were blamed when their graduates could not find jobs. Public school administrators were blamed when their graduates could not handle jobs. Both groups acknowledged the problems, took charge, and promised to devise expeditious solutions.

LAW SCHOOL ADMINISTRATORS DODGE ACCUSATIONS

Students in law school realized that their training would be expensive. Although some of them had to take out massive loans, they did not panic. They expected to pay them off after they secured high-salaried jobs.

The administrators at the law schools had told prospective students about the ease with which recent graduates had landed choice jobs. They convinced them that that they would be just as successful (Mikoulianitch, 2012).

The students eventually began to doubt the assurances of the administrators. In fact, they had become genuinely anxious by 2010. They were questioning whether they would be able to find any sort of legal job.

The anxious students were prescient: many of them could not find positions. They then went back to their law school administrators. They reminded them of the recruitment pitches that they had made and the employment prospects that they had described.

The administrators were philosophical with the graduates. They observed that all careers had fluctuating patterns of employment. They stated that legal careers, which had been robust for decades, would recover soon. They encouraged the graduates to be patient.

The administrators had some practical tips for graduates. They counseled them to be alert to the full range of employment opportunities. They explained that they should consider not only the high-salaried jobs in large firms and corporations but also the modest-salaried positions in courts, public agencies, and nonprofit organizations.

The unemployed graduates followed the administrators' advice. They kept their eyes open for all sorts of jobs. Moreover, they were extremely patient.

The graduates remained watchful and patient for years. However, they eventually returned to the administrators. They told them that they were anxious because they still were unemployed. They confessed that they had become more anxious after they discovered that half of recent law school graduates were in the same predicament. They concluded that the legal job market had not improved or shown any signs of improving (Harper, 2015; Kessenides, 2014).

The graduates were upset with the law school administrators. They berated them for continuing to recruit students as aggressively as they ever had. They noted that they even had lowered academic admission standards to fill classes.

The graduates were disillusioned with the law school administrators. They concluded that they had no interest in helping them. They looked for another group with which to confide their problems. They went to journalists.

The graduates told the journalists about their employment problems and the way the administrators were behaving. They hoped that they would get this information to any individuals who were contemplating legal careers (Campos, 2014; Milne-Tyte, 2014).

Some of the graduates came up with an additional way to get publicity. They set up websites on which they personally recounted their experiences with unethical law school administrators (Forgotten Attorney, 2015; Form Tool, 2015; Fuchs, 2013; Unemployed Lawyer, 2011; Zaretsky, 2015).

Some graduates detected still another way to get publicity. Having been taught to sue persons who misled clients, they sued their former administrators for misleading them.

Enthusiasts

The law school administrators initially had ignored graduates when they posed troublesome questions. They had used the same strategy when journalists posed questions. However, they soon realized that this strategy was not working.

The administrators announced that they would be responding to the questions from graduates and journalists. They began by answering their question about the number of persons who had completed law school and then found jobs (Chow, 2012).

The administrators were well aware that the graduates and the journalists already had data indicating serious employment problems. However, they contended that these data, which had been nationally aggregated, misrepresented the situations at individual law schools.

The administrators were going to tabulate separate employment statistics for each law school. They explained that these statistics would inform prospective applicants about their job prospects at particular institutions.

The administrators hoped that their plan would mollify disgruntled graduates, satisfy inquisitive journalists, and divert curious members of the public. Most important of all, they hoped that it would persuade aspiring lawyers to keep enrolling in their programs.

Skeptics

The administrators posted employment statistics for each law school. They believed that these customized figures gave applicants reason to be confident.

Disgruntled graduates were initially confused by the administrators' employment figures. They wondered why they were so different from their own figures.

When the law school administrators had made calculations, they had included data about former students who had been hired into short-term positions at their own law schools. They contended that these students were employed within the legal profession (Chow, 2012).

The graduates still were disgruntled. They explained that they had expected data about former students who had been hired into jobs that required legal degrees, that were full-time, and that were permanent. They were miffed when they realized that they had been given different data.

The disgruntled graduates believed that the administrators had been disingenuous. However, they needed help to expose their ruse. They again went to journalists.

The journalists sympathized with the disgruntled graduates. They agreed with them that the administrators had supplied misinformation. Moreover, they believed that they had supplied it deliberately. They agreed to help the graduates (*New York Times* Editorial Board, 2015b).

PUBLIC SCHOOL ADMINISTRATORS DODGE ACCUSATIONS

George W. Bush and Barack Obama represented different political parties. Nonetheless, they had remarkably similar beliefs about education.

The two presidents agreed that the nation's public schools were in serious trouble. They also agreed that school administrators were to blame.

The presidents presented their views to federal legislators, governors, and state legislators. They cited low scores on commercial standardized tests as evidence. They demanded that the school administrators do more to raise those scores.

The school administrators were not impressed. They had little confidence in the commercial standardized tests about which the politicians were ranting. In fact, they wished to reduce the number of these tests that their students were completing (Giordano, 2016).

The politicians replied that they had full confidence in commercial standardized tests. They had no interest in reducing their number. Quite the opposite, they wished to expand that number dramatically.

The politicians had another way they were going to demonstrate their confidence in tests: they wished to make school administrators directly accountable for the scores on them. They explained that they would use the scores to differentiate effective from ineffective administrators.

The politicians had attempted to place rhetorical pressure on the school administrators. They were annoyed when the administrators did not respond enthusiastically to it. However, they intended to apply another type of pressure on them. They were going to adjust the funding to their schools on the bases of students' test scores.

Enthusiasts

The politicians were excited about their plan to link funding to test scores. They expected it to be popular with some groups. They were sure that it would be popular with members of the business community.

Businesspeople had for decades decried public school graduates. They complained that they could not handle the responsibilities for the jobs into which they were hired (Giordano, 2000, 2003, 2009, 2010, 2011, 2012b).

The businesspeople applauded the politicians for trying to raise students' test scores. They agreed with them that higher scores would lead to better workers.

The businesspeople also liked the politicians' strategy of making school administrators accountable for low test scores. They noted that this strategy was similar to that on which they relied in industry and commerce. They explained that they held middle-level managers accountable when workers failed to reach performance targets.

Those businesspeople who sold educational technology showed a particularly keen interest in the new education plan. They agreed with the politicians that attention to testing was visionary. However, they encouraged them to expand their vision to include educational technology.

The businesspeople who sold educational technology reminded the politicians of the campaign contributions that they had given to them. They confided that they were ready to give still more. However, they expected a payback: they wanted greater public spending on products from their firms.

The politicians were willing to increase technology spending. However, they anticipated that skeptical constituents would pepper them with troublesome questions. They asked the businesspeople to supply them with rejoinders for these questions.

The technology businesspeople agreed to give the politicians help. After all, they realized that it would be to their self-interest.

The businesspeople articulated potent arguments to justify spending on educational technology. They stated that students needed experience with technology to qualify for digital jobs. They added that they also needed it to participate fully in a digital society.

The businesspeople had still one more argument to justify public spending on educational technology. They noted that the government already was spending large sums purchasing, administering, scoring, and disseminating the results of commercial tests. They contended that technology would reduce these expenses (Miller & McVee, 2012; Ribble, 2011).

Politicians wished to be responsive to the technology businesspeople. Even the president expressed this wish. President Obama announced that he would be expanding technology-based testing, technology-based instruction, and the high-speed scholastic Internet services that these initiatives required. He assumed that businesspeople would be pleased by these plans. He was correct.

Although businesspeople were pleased with Obama, school administrators were not. They were blindsided by the announcement that he would be expanding technology-based testing. They reminded him of his campaign pledge to restrict this type of testing (Giordano, 2015, 2016).

Political candidates in both parties kept their eyes on Obama. They watched as he increased public funding on educational technology. They also watched as he skillfully engendered public support for those increases.

Most candidates who were competing in the 2016 presidential election repeated Obama's pledge to spend heavily on educational technology. For example, Jeb Bush, who was one of the contenders, bragged about the way he had expanded computer-assisted testing and computer-assisted instruction when he was governor of Florida. He told voters that he would replicate those initiatives nationwide (Bush, 2016; "Jeb Bush on Education," 2015; Mencimer, 2011).

Governor Chris Christie was another presidential contender in 2016. Like Jeb Bush, he intended to increase public spending on educational technology. However, he had a simpler plan than that of Bush: he would buy an iPad for every public school student in the nation (Neff, 2015).

The school administrators listened when politicians pledged to spend more on educational technology. They did not doubt that they were providing corporate donors with paybacks. Nonetheless, they were not completely unhappy. After all, they realized that the politicians were providing them with opportunities to reduce some of the pressure that they were feeling.

The school administrators told the politicians and businesspeople that they approved of plans to escalate technology. They especially liked Christie's proposal to provide federal funds for iPads. They agreed with him that this spending would increase students' job readiness. In fact, they would go forward with this proposal even before they had federal funds.

School administrators had a clever way to get money for iPads: they would adopt digital textbooks. They contended that these books created savings because they were less expensive than printed books. They intended to use the savings to offset the purchase costs of iPads (Hennick, 2013).

School administrators wished to get parents behind their technology initiatives. They assured them that iPads and digital textbooks would accelerate children's academic progress. However, they anticipated that some parents still would be anxious.

School administrators were not surprised when some of the parents questioned whether their children would be able to use iPads. They told them that their children would get used to their iPads quickly because they would be relying on them not only to read e-textbooks but also to conduct classroom research, communicate, and write (Hennick, 2013; Nichols, 2013).

School administrators anticipated that parents would be anxious because they personally were unfamiliar with iPads. They told them to be at ease because they would be given opportunities to learn about the devices (Blume, 2014; Webster, 2015).

School administrators anticipated that parents would be apprehensive about the ability of some teachers to adapt to iPad-based instruction. They told them that even inexperienced teachers would have little trouble because they would be mentored by technology-savvy peers (Gliksman, 2013; Martinez, 2010).

As for the teachers, some of them were genuinely excited about iPads. They were convinced that the students who already had these devices at home would quickly discover ways to use them at school; they predicted that even students who did not have iPads at home would become proficient because they would be so fascinated by the novel technology ("iPad Management," 2013; Willis, 2013).

Skeptics

Parents conceded that iPads would be easy to operate and stimulating. They also conceded that they would prepare children for technology-based jobs. Nonetheless, they still had reservations about plans to purchase a device for every child.

The skeptical parents contended that many children already spent too much time interacting with iPads in their homes. They preferred that they use school time to interact directly with teachers and peers (Pogue, 2011; Rimel, 2014; Walters, 2015).

The superintendent of a large California school district did not wish to haggle with skeptical parents. He told them that he was ready to give every child an iPad (Jacobs, 2014).

Some of the parents were intrigued by this superintendent's initiative. Nonetheless, they grimaced when they learned that it would require more than a billion dollars. They encouraged him to deliberate carefully before making this expenditure.

Parents made counter suggestions when their superintendents were going to spend enormous amounts on iPads. They suggested that they instead repair shoddy facilities, replace obsolete equipment, increase school safety, or hire critical instructional personnel (Hennick, 2013; Murphy, 2014).

The skeptical parents asked teachers to collaborate with them on spending priorities. They were pleased when many of them agreed to join them.

The teachers cooperated with the parents because they sympathized with them. They also cooperated because they detected conflicts of interest among the politicians and businesspeople who were promoting educational technology (Giordano, 2016).

EXAMINING EVASIVE RESPONSES

Law school administrators were chastised for recruiting students who could not find jobs. Public school administrators were chastised for preparing students who could not succeed in jobs. One group tried to silence critics by giving students temporary jobs; the other tried to quiet them by giving students iPads.

Activity 8.1

When law school administrators were asked about students' employment rates, they traditionally had highlighted only those graduates with permanent jobs. How did groups respond?

Table 8.1 identifies two groups: law school graduates and journalists.

Complete the table by indicating the ways in which the groups responded to the administrators. You can use symbols.

Use the symbol − if the groups expressed low confidence in them. Use the symbol ± for moderate confidence and the symbol + for high confidence. As a final step, explain the bases for the symbols that you selected.

You can rely on the information in this chapter, additional information, or the information cited in the references. If you are reading this chapter with colleagues, you can confer with them.

Table 8.1. Law School Administrators Highlight Graduates with Permanent Jobs

Groups	Response*	Explanation
Graduates		
Journalists		

*− Low
± Moderate
+ High

Activity 8.2

When law school administrators were asked about students' employment rates, they began to highlight even those graduates with temporary jobs. How did groups respond?

Table 8.2 identifies two groups: law school graduates and journalists.

Complete the table by indicating the ways in which the groups responded to the administrators. You can use symbols.

Use the symbol − if the groups expressed low confidence in them. Use the symbol ± for moderate confidence and the symbol + for high confidence. As a final step, explain the bases for the symbols that you selected.

Who Should Take Charge of School Technology? 85

Table 8.2. **Law School Administrators Highlight Graduates with Temporary Jobs**

Groups	Response*	Explanation
Graduates		
Journalists		

*– Low
± Moderate
+ High

Activity 8.3

When public school administrators were asked about students' job readiness, they traditionally had highlighted their test scores. How did groups respond?

Table 8.3 identifies two groups: businesspeople and parents.

Complete the table by indicating the ways in which the groups responded to the administrators. You can use symbols.

Use the symbol – if the groups expressed low confidence in them. Use the symbol ± for moderate confidence and the symbol + for high confidence. As a final step, explain the bases for the symbols that you selected.

Table 8.3. **Public School Administrators Highlight Students' Test Scores**

Groups	Response*	Explanation
Businesspeople		
Parents		

*– Low
± Moderate
+ High

Activity 8.4

When public school administrators were asked about students' job readiness, they began to highlight their access to iPads. How did groups respond?

Table 8.4 identifies two groups: businesspeople and parents.

Complete the table by indicating the ways in which the groups responded to the administrators. You can use symbols.

Use the symbol – if the groups expressed low confidence in them. Use the symbol ± for moderate confidence and the symbol + for high confidence. As a final step, explain the bases for the symbols that you selected.

Table 8.4. Public School Administrators Highlight Students' Access to iPads

Groups	Response*	Explanation
Businesspeople		
Parents		

*– Low
± Moderate
+ High

SUMMARY

Law school administrators were chastised for recruiting students who could not find jobs. Public school administrators were chastised for preparing students who could not succeed in jobs. One group responded by giving students temporary jobs; the other responded by giving them iPads.

Chapter 9

Who Should Take Charge of Privatizing Public Schools?

If 51 percent of [the parents at a California school] sign a [trigger law] petition, they can demand . . . a new set of administrators . . .[or] a charter school operator.
—Peg Tyre, 2011

[The trigger law] was developed . . . by parents, legislators, and a grassroots non-profit.
—StudentsFirst Vice President Eric Lerum, 2012

If you're against [the trigger law], you're against parent power.
—Parent Revolution Leader Ben Austen,
quoted by Yarbrough, 2013

Critics argue the [trigger] law is a corporate-backed privatization tool under the guise of parent empowerment.
—Natasha Lindstrom, 2014

School administrators allowed teachers to handle violent students. Politicians allowed schoolboards to handle school privatization. However, both groups alleged that they were under pressure to take charge of and make changes to these procedures.

GRASSROOTS PRESSURE TO DISCIPLINE VIOLENT STUDENTS

Parents were shocked when children were threatened or assaulted at school. They asked school administrators to take steps to keep them safe (Almond, 2008; Lysiak, 2013).

The school administrators replied that children already were safe at school. They explained that they were protected by their teachers. They encouraged the teachers to be on the lookout for threatening situations and then use their discretion about the best way to intervene.

The administrators directed teachers to employ progressive disciplinary practices with violent students. For example, they instructed the teachers to moderately punish those who made verbal threats but severely punish those who followed through on threats (Parks, 2009).

The school administrators had hoped that parents would be soothed by progressive disciplinary measures. However, they acknowledged that some of them were still anxious. They therefore turned to more extreme measures.

School administrators adopted no-tolerance practices. They explained that the new practices required their staffs to apply the identical punishment to all misbehaving students. They typically required them to suspend students who committed major or minor infractions (May, 2014).

The school administrators had shifted the way that they were handling school threats. They hoped that parents would be pleased. However, they discovered that many parents were not even aware of the shift. They asked journalists for help informing them.

The journalists were eager to report about no-tolerance policies and practices. However, they concentrated on cases in which students brought guns to school and were then suspended. They ignored the many students who committed minor infractions and were suspended (Lieberman, 2008).

Enthusiasts

The school administrators were proud of their no-tolerance practices. They noted that they prevented teachers from employing discretion and being too lenient with violent or potentially violent students. They boasted that they made students safer.

Teachers who worked at schools with no-tolerance policies meted out severe punishments to all misbehaving students. As they had done historically, they suspended students who brought guns to school. However, they now suspended those who brought toy guns. In some cases, they suspended those who made gun-like gestures (May, 2014).

Some persons were upset with the school administrators. They claimed that they were acting autocratically. They faulted them for failing to consult with parents.

The school administrators retorted that they had not been autocratic. They contended that they had made changes in response to grassroots pressure from parents.

Skeptics

Some parents did support the school administrators. However, they later became skeptical.

Parents complained that the school administrators had not explained the full ramifications of no-tolerance practices. They were surprised at the many students whom they were suspending for minor misbehaviors. They pleaded for a return to progressive disciplinary practices (May, 2014).

The disgruntled parents were unable to persuade the school administrators to restore progressive disciplinary practices. They therefore went to journalists and asked them to report about children who were being mistreated. They urged them to recruit sympathizers from their readers, listeners, and viewers.

The journalists listened to the parents. They were intrigued because they were complaining about safety policies and practices that the school administrators had attributed to them.

The journalists decided that they would investigate the students who were being suspended. They readily found cases in which these students posed threats and deserved to be suspended. However, they also found cases in which they seemed to have been treated inappropriately.

The journalists noted a troublesome pattern among the students who had been suspended: a disproportionately high number of them represented racial and ethnic minorities. They questioned whether the no-tolerance practices were fostering discrimination (Abdullah, 2014; Daniels, 2009).

The journalists arrived at another troublesome conclusion: school administrators had devised no-tolerance practices that prevented their staffs from employing any type of discretion whatsoever. The journalists used examples to underscore this contention.

In one example, school administrators had witnessed a five-year-old who was describing a pink plastic toy gun with which she blew bubbles. They suspended her and required her to undergo a psychological evaluation before she could return to school.

When the school administrators were challenged, they explained that the girl's comments could have been construed as terrorist threats. They believed that their parent-approved no-tolerance policy left them no alternative other than to treat her in the way that they had (Reynolds, 2013).

The journalists reported at length about the school administrators who had disciplined the bubble-blowing five-year-old girl. They must have assumed that they never would find a case that was more bizarre. However, they changed their minds after they learned about a seven-year-old boy in Maryland.

The Maryland youngster had been nibbling at a pop-tart at lunchtime. When he was quizzed about the shape of the tart, he replied that it was a mountain.

A teacher on cafeteria duty heard the boy's response. However, she did not believe him. She was convinced that he was sculpting his pop-tart into a gun.

The teacher consulted with her principal. The two of them concluded that their district's no-tolerance policy required them to send this boy home (Mangu-Ward, 2013).

Scores of journalists publicized the boy's suspension. They also publicized a proposed Florida law intended to prevent additional suspensions of this sort. They waggishly referred to this legislation as the "pop-tart law" (Pillow, 2014).

GRASSROOTS PRESSURE TO PRIVATIZE PUBLIC SCHOOLS

At the end of the twentieth century, many politicians were displeased with the federal government's educational policies. Although they wanted to make alterations to them, they could not agree.

The politicians bickered publicly for decades. When Republicans made proposals, Democrats dismissed them as partisan. However, Republicans greeted Democratic proposals in the same fashion.

Although the two parties had seemed irreconcilable, they surprised everyone in 2001. They announced that they had come up with mutually acceptable changes to the federal government's educational policies.

The politicians were relieved that they had crafted a bipartisan plan. Nonetheless, they were anxious about how constituents would react to it. They were particularly nervous about the way businesspeople would respond.

The businesspeople stated that they would support the new plan. Some of them had a selfish reason: they detected financial opportunities. They were especially impressed by the opportunities to create entrepreneurial schools.

The politicians were gratified that business constituents detected benefits. Nonetheless, they did not want to flaunt those benefits. They worried that parents would be suspicious of a plan that treated businesspeople too generously.

The politicians resolved to be careful. They demonstrated that care even when they were selecting a name for their plan. They wanted one that would obfuscate rather than highlight its business benefits. They eventually made the perfect choice: they called it the No Child Left Behind Act (Giordano, 2007, 2009).

Enthusiasts

Some business executives were excited about the No Child Left Behind Act. Those who were establishing for-profit schools were extremely excited. They realized that the legislation gave them unprecedented chances to expand their market.

Even though the executives at for-profit schools detected rich opportunities, some of them still were not satisfied. Those in California were irked by the procedures they had to follow when they were advancing proposals to establish new school sites.

The executives explained that they had to submit proposals to local schoolboards. They complained that these boards demonstrated enormous discretion. They noted that they not only deliberated at length but also sometimes rejected their proposals.

The executives asked California's legislators to supplement the No Child Left Behind law with a state law. They explained that they wanted a state law that would prevent the schoolboards from blocking their efforts to privatize public schools. They wanted a fast-track approval procedure.

The legislators had no objection to fast-track approval. Nonetheless, they worried how parents would react to it. They needed an engaging and easy-to-grasp rationale to present to them. They asked the executives to provide one.

The executives came up with an explanation that was somewhat circuitous. Nonetheless, they believed that it still was persuasive. They explained that parents could use the fast-track school privatization law to fire and replace ineffective principals. They reasoned that the parents therefore were the primary beneficiaries.

The executives believed that their argument would be enhanced by a chilling metaphor. They depicted ineffective principals as lame horses. They argued that parents should be able to point a pistol at them, pull the trigger, and prevent them from causing additional misery.

The California legislators liked the rationale that the executives had provided. They announced that they were ready to confront ineffective principals. They defined ineffective principals as those who supervised schools with multiyear records of low test scores (California Department of Education, 2014).

The California legislators passed their bill in 2010. As had been the case with the federal legislators who had passed the No Child Left Behind law, they wanted an endearing name for their law. Insisting that their law was designed to make principals accountable to parents, they christened it the Parent Empowerment Act.

Supporters ignored the name that the legislators had selected. Unable to disassociate the law from the lame-horse metaphor, they preferred to call it the trigger law.

Parents could use the trigger law to rapidly make changes at low-performing schools. For example, they needed only a majority to fire the administrative staff at any of these schools (California Department of Education, 2014).

After the parents had "pulled the trigger" on the administrators, they would replace them. If they wanted a new slate of public school administrators, they would present this demand to their local schoolboard (McGray, 2009).

The parents did not have to settle for public school personnel. They had another option: they could demand private-sector managers. They could present this demand to a for-profit educational firm (McGray, 2009).

The executives at the for-profit educational firms were excited about the trigger law. They realized that it gave them a way to bypass local schoolboards.

The executives expected that schoolboards would become weaker and that their firms would grow stronger. However, they realized that some schoolboards still could retaliate. They worried that they would try to bolster their power by enlisting parents and the general public as allies.

The executives wished to make it harder for the schoolboards to gather allies. They asked journalists to help them discredit the boards. They urged them to editorialize about the tyrannical manner in which the boards exercised discretion.

Some journalists were eager to assist the executives. They agreed with them that the California schoolboards had far too much power. They praised the trigger law for taking away some of that power and giving it to parents (Maxwell, 2009; Tyre, 2011; Wood, 2010).

Legislators in Connecticut, Indiana, Louisiana, Mississippi, Texas, and Ohio were impressed by California's trigger law. They were especially impressed by the way that it had been attributed to parents. They claimed that they were under pressure from parents in their states to create similar laws (Cunningham, 2013).

Skeptics

Some Californians were annoyed after their legislators explained the trigger law. They believed that they had "astroturfed" it to give the illusion that it was inspired by a grassroots movement (Rizga, 2011).

California's public school educators were particularly incensed. They thought that the legislators had misrepresented parents' attitudes toward their schoolboards.

The educators doubted that parents disapproved of the deliberative manner in which schoolboards made decisions. They could not imagine why they would want the boards to use less discretion. They urged their unions to meet with parents and ascertain their genuine feelings (Grannan, 2012).

California's schoolboards were even more skeptical. They were skeptical of the legislators' alleged motives. They believed that they had been responding to pressure from the for-profit educational firms rather than the parents. They pointed out that they had crafted the trigger law to benefit those firms.

Many California parents were angry with the legislators who had enacted the trigger law. They were convinced that they had damaged public schools and the students at them. Although they were upset with them for passing the law, they were even more upset with them for attributing it to parents (Grannan, 2012; "Parent-Trigger War," 2012).

EXAMINING ASSERTIONS ABOUT GRASSROOTS ACTIVISM

School administrators made contentious scholastic changes. When they were challenged, they insisted that they had been following grassroots advice from parents. They made an impression on politicians, who used the same rationale to justify contentious scholastic changes.

Activity 9.1

School administrators traditionally had delegated broad authority to teachers. They encouraged them to use discretion with violent or potentially violent students. How did groups respond?

Table 9.1 identifies two groups: teachers and parents.

Complete the table by indicating the ways in which the groups responded to the school administrators. You can use symbols.

Use the symbol – if the groups exhibited low confidence. Use the symbol ± for moderate confidence and the symbol + for high confidence. As a final step, explain the bases for the symbols that you selected.

You can rely on the information in this chapter, additional information, or the information cited in the references. If you are reading this chapter with colleagues, you can confer with them.

Table 9.1. School Administrators Delegate Disciplinary Authority to Teachers

Groups	Response*	Explanation
Teachers		
Parents		

*– Low
± Moderate
+ High

Activity 9.2

School administrators contended that they were under grassroots pressure to limit teachers' authority. They enacted no-tolerance policies to prevent teachers from using discretion with violent or potentially violent students. How did groups respond?

Table 9.2 identifies two groups: teachers and parents.

Complete the table by indicating the ways in which the groups responded to the school administrators. You can use symbols.

Use the symbol – if the groups exhibited low confidence. Use the symbol ± for moderate confidence and the symbol + for high confidence. As a final step, explain the bases for the symbols that you selected.

Table 9.2. School Administrators Limit the Disciplinary Authority of Teachers

Groups	Response*	Explanation
Teachers		
Parents		

*– Low
± Moderate
+ High

Activity 9.3

California's legislators traditionally had delegated broad authority to local schoolboards. They encouraged them to use discretion with proposals to privatize public schools. How did groups respond?

Table 9.3 identifies two groups: local schoolboards and parents.

Complete the table by indicating the ways in which the groups responded to the legislators. You can use symbols.

Use the symbol – if the groups exhibited low confidence. Use the symbol ± for moderate confidence and the symbol + for high confidence. As a final step, explain the bases for the symbols that you selected.

Who Should Take Charge of Privatizing Public Schools? 95

Table 9.3. California Legislators Give Schoolboards Authority for Privatizing Public Schools

Groups	Response*	Explanation
School Boards		
Parents		

*– Low
± Moderate
+ High

Activity 9.4

California's legislators contended that they were under grassroots pressure to limit local schoolboards' authority. They enacted the trigger law to prevent schoolboards from using discretion with proposals to privatize public schools. How did groups respond?

Table 9.4 identifies two groups: local schoolboards and parents.

Complete the table by indicating the ways in which the groups responded to the legislators. You can use symbols.

Use the symbol – if the groups exhibited low confidence. Use the symbol ± for moderate confidence and the symbol + for high confidence. As a final step, explain the bases for the symbols that you selected.

Table 9.4. California Legislators Limit Schoolboards' Authority for Privatizing Public Schools

Groups	Response*	Explanation
School Boards		
Parents		

*– Low
± Moderate
+ High

SUMMARY

School administrators made controversial scholastic changes. When they were challenged, they insisted that they had followed the grassroots advice of parents. They inspired politicians to use the same rationalization for some of the controversial scholastic changes that they made.

Chapter 10

Who Should Take Charge of Tests?

[I was required to give a test that was] written on a fifth-grade level . . . [to a student who was] reading on a first-grade level.
—New York Special Education Teacher Brian Zorn, 2015

[As a parent,] you have the right to opt your child out of [inappropriate] tests.
—New York State United Teachers, 2015a

We hope you'll opt [your child] out of [inappropriate] tests.
—New York Parent Heather Roberts, quoted by Harris & Fessenden, 2015

[New York's] schools are now confronting a full-fledged "opt-out movement."
—Ben Zimmer, 2015

Consumers were upset about unwanted telemarketing calls. Parents were upset about unwanted school tests. Both groups expressed their frustration, took charge, and rebelled.

REBEL CONSUMERS

Marketers needed clients from retailing. They tried to lure them with promises to increase their sales.

After they had attracted clients, the marketers had to follow through on their promises. They typically relied on a three-stage strategy: they fashioned persuasive sales pitches, incorporated them into ads, and then displayed the ads where consumers would notice them.

The marketers were always on the lookout for new ways to get the attention of consumers. Some of them hired agents to go door to door and contact them at home. Others came up with a less expensive option: they phoned them (Bencin & Jonovic, 1989; McHatton, 1988).

Enthusiasts

The marketers referred to phone-based advertising as telemarketing. They initially used it occasionally. After they confirmed that it was effective, they began to use it more and more (Stone & Wyman, 1992).

The marketers never doubted their new strategy's effectiveness. Nonetheless, they discovered that many consumers were complaining about it. As a result, they did doubt their new strategy's long-term prospects.

The marketers were not sure how to handle the grumbling consumers. They therefore requested advice from their professional association—the Direct Marketing Association (DMA).

The DMA's leaders came up with a simple solution: they would create a no-call list for consumers. They then would direct their members to avoid calling any persons who placed their names on this list (Direct Marketing Association, 2015).

Skeptics

Consumers had to pay a fee to register for the DMA's no-call list. Although they may have been irked by the expense, they still looked forward to the benefits.

Consumers eventually became disillusioned with the no-call list. They noted that they still were receiving many calls. In fact, they judged that they were receiving as many as they had before they had placed their names on the list.

The consumers realized that the marketers had not solved their problem. They did not believe that they would solve it. They therefore went to federal legislators and asked for their help opting out of annoying calls.

The legislators listened sympathetically to the distraught consumers. Although they claimed that they were concerned about unwanted calling, they did not take any steps to restrict it.

The consumers wondered whether another group would be more helpful. This time, they went to journalists. They asked them to report about irresponsible telemarketing practices. They hoped that they would pressure the legislators into action.

The telemarketers recognized that consumers wished to regulate their industry. They insisted that they could self-regulate it. They stated that they already had taken a significant step by compiling a no-call list. Although they acknowledged that this list had been problematic, they were confident that they could improve it.

Consumers were exasperated with the telemarketers' no-call list. They wanted legislators to establish a separate, government-monitored list.

The legislators had underestimated their constituents. Once they realized how upset they were, they assured them that they were ready to act. They pledged that they would establish a new no-call list.

The legislators established the new no-call list in 2003. They dubbed it the *Do Not Call Registry*. They directed the Federal Trade Commission to identify any advertising agencies that were ignoring it and impose stiff civil penalties on them (Federal Trade Commission, 2015a; U.S. Government, 2015).

Consumers were enthusiastic about the federal government's *Do Not Call Registry*. In a very short time, more than 50 percent of those with phones had placed their names on it (Federal Trade Commission, 2015b).

REBEL PARENTS

George W. Bush hoped to follow Bill Clinton into the White House. However, he worried that he would not get the votes that he would require.

Bush used political promises to get more votes. For example, he promised that he would do more for the schools than Clinton had.

Bush claimed that Clinton had mishandled the schools. He was miffed by the way Clinton had dealt with tests. Bush noted that Clinton had recommended only three of them: one in elementary school, another in middle school, and one more in high school (Aldeman, 2015).

Bush claimed that Clinton also had mishandled school resources. Bush stated that Clinton had distributed them without holding educators accountable for them.

Bush had very different attitudes toward educational tests and educational resources. He explained that he would require more tests. He added that he then would use the scores from them as a basis for allocating resources.

Enthusiasts

Bush won the presidential election. He attributed some of his success to his school reform pledges.

Bush had provided scant details about how students would be affected by his reform pledges. Although he had said that students would have to complete more tests, he never disclosed the precise number.

Bush eventually did identify the number of tests that children would have to complete. He embedded that figure within the 2001 No Child Left Behind law. He stated that children would have to complete seventeen tests (Giordano, 2005, 2009).

Bush had specified that children would have to complete seventeen federally mandated tests. However, he noted that they would have to complete any additional tests that their individual states required (Bidwell, 2015; Wallace, 2015).

Parents were anxious about the new federal tests. They had many practical questions about them. For example, they inquired about their lengths, their formats, their content, the grades in which they would be administered, and the ways that the scores from them would be used.

Parents also were anxious about new state tests. They requested details about them from their governors, state legislators, and state educational officials.

Parents in New York went to their regents for information about state tests. They realized that the members of this group had extraordinary power over schools.

The regents told the parents that they did intend to supplement the seventeen federal tests with additional state tests. However, they had to determine how many more state tests they would require.

The regents stated that they were struggling to determine the number of state tests because they would be using them in an unprecedented fashion. They would be relying on them to assess not only students but also teachers and school administrators.

Skeptics

New York's parents were anxious about the tests that the president and members of Congress required. They were just as anxious about those that their regents were getting ready to require. They wanted details, and they wanted them quickly.

The regents replied that they could not yet give the parents the information that they had requested. However, they gave them some limited information about the new state tests. They hoped that it would appease them.

The regents pledged to the parents that the content on the new tests would reflect material that had been introduced within their children's classrooms. They also pledged that passing scores would reflect the abilities of local students. Finally, they pledged that the consequences for failure would reflect the concerns of local parents.

Many of the parents did not trust the regents to honor their assurances. They still wanted them to delay their testing plans.

The regents ignored the troublesome parents. They stated that they would commission special state tests. They added that they had complete confidence in them.

Even though the regents claimed to have had confidence in their tests, they apparently lost it. They concluded that these tests did not enable them to manage the schools. They explained that they were not rigorous enough to meet their evolving needs.

The regents announced that they were replacing their current tests with a new generation of tests. They would be commissioning Common Core tests (Giordano, 2016).

The regents described how Common Core tests differed from current tests. They noted that they had content that was more challenging. They added that they had passing scores that were more difficult to achieve. Finally, they noted that they had high-stakes consequence for students, teachers, and school administrators (Brody, 2015; *Newsday* Editorial Board, 2015).

The parents were anxious about the new tests. They had numerous questions about them. They posed them directly to the regents.

- How much time would their children spend preparing for the new tests?
- How much time would they spend taking them?
- How would they benefit from them?
- What were the prices of the tests?
- What were the motives of the businesspeople who promoted the tests?
- What were the motives of the regents who advocated them?
- How closely would the content on the tests match that of classroom instruction?
- How closely would the format of the tests match that in their children's textbooks, workbooks, and digital learning materials?
- Would scores be affected when the tests were computer-administered?
- Would they be affected by the test-taking strategies with which children had been drilled?
- Would they be affected by student penalties?
- Would they be affected by teacher penalties?
- How much blame did children deserve for low scores?
- How much blame did teachers deserve?
- How much blame did school administrators deserve?
- How much blame did the regents deserve?

The parents believed that they were posing common sense queries. They expected straightforward answers. When they did not get them, they were furious.

The parents announced that they would not support the new statewide emphasis on testing. They were sure that it would harm their children. They were ready to rebel (Cassidy, 2015; National Center for Fair and Open Testing, 2015).

Teachers sympathized with the rebel parents. They assured them that they had the right to protect their children from irresponsible testing. They also assured them that they would be assisted by their union—New York State United Teachers (New York State United Teachers, 2015a; NYS ALLIES for Public Education, 2015).

The teachers' union gave the parents practical assistance. For example, it supplied them with a letter that they could give to administrators. This letter gave directions about how the administrators should classify "opt-out" students.

> I am writing to respectfully inform you that my child . . . will be scored as a "refusal". . . . Please note that a "refusal" is *not* the same as "absent" as they are defined differently and scored with different standard achieved codes. (NYS ALLIES for Public Education, 2015)

Some school administrators were annoyed when the parents presented letters from the union. They told them that they were being hoodwinked by this organization. They warned that they were harming their children (Esmonde, 2015; Wallace, 2015).

The opt-out parents were not surprised when school administrators attacked them, the teachers, and the union. However, they were shocked when they attacked children. They fumed when they forced students to "sit and stare" at their desktops throughout entire testing sessions (Harris, 2015b; Tata & Ford, 2014).

The parents wanted to restrain retaliatory school administrators. However, they needed a strategy. They returned to the teachers' union for more assistance.

The union created another printed message that opt-out parents could present to school administrators. The message stated that their children would attend school on testing dates only if they were provided with educationally suitable activities (NYS ALLIES for Public Education, 2015).

EXAMINING QUESTIONS FROM REBELS

Consumers were upset about unwanted telemarketing calls. Parents were upset about unwanted school tests. The two groups expressed their frustration, took charge, and rebelled.

Activity 10.1

Marketers used telephone advertising. However, they initially used it infrequently. How did groups respond?

Table 10.1 identifies two groups: the clients whom the marketers represented and the consumers whom they targeted.

Complete the table by indicating the ways in which the groups responded to the marketers. You can use symbols.

Use the symbol – if the groups expressed low confidence in them. Use the symbol ± for moderate confidence and the symbol + for high confidence. As a final step, explain the bases for the symbols that you selected.

You can rely on the information in this chapter, additional information, or the information cited in the references. If you are reading this chapter with colleagues, you can confer with them.

Table 10.1. Marketers Use Phone Ads Infrequently

Groups	Response*	Explanation
Clients		
Consumers		

*– Low
± Moderate
+ High

Activity 10.2

Marketers began to use telephone advertising more frequently. How did groups respond?

Table 10.2 identifies two groups: the clients whom the marketers represented and the consumers whom they targeted.

Complete the table by indicating the ways in which the groups responded to the marketers. You can use symbols.

Use the symbol – if the groups expressed low confidence in them. Use the symbol ± for moderate confidence and the symbol + for high confidence. As a final step, explain the bases for the symbols that you selected.

Table 10.2. Marketers Use Phone Ads Frequently

Groups	Response*	Explanation
Clients		
Consumers		

* − Low
± Moderate
+ High

Activity 10.3

New York's regents administered tests. However, they initially administered them infrequently. How did groups respond?

Table 10.3 identifies two New York groups: parents and teachers.

Complete the table by indicating the ways in which the groups responded to the regents. You can use symbols.

Use the symbol − if the groups expressed low confidence in them. Use the symbol ± for moderate confidence and the symbol + for high confidence. As a final step, explain the bases for the symbols that you selected.

Table 10.3. New York's Regents Administer Tests Infrequently

Groups	Response*	Explanation
Parents		
Teachers		

* − Low
± Moderate
+ High

Activity 10.4

New York's regents began to administer tests more frequently. How did groups respond?

Table 10.4 identifies two New York groups: parents and teachers.

Complete the table by indicating the ways in which the groups responded to the regents. You can use symbols.

Use the symbol – if the groups expressed low confidence in them. Use the symbol ± for moderate confidence and the symbol + for high confidence. As a final step, explain the bases for the symbols that you selected.

Table 10.4. New York's Regents Administer Tests Frequently

Groups	Response*	Explanation
Parents		
Teachers		

* – Low
± Moderate
+ High

SUMMARY

Consumers were upset about unwanted telemarketing calls. Parents were upset about unwanted school tests. Both groups took action: they rebelled.

References

Abdullah, H. (2014, January 30). Minority kids disproportionately impacted by zero-tolerance laws. Cnn.com. Retrieved from: http://www.cnn.com/2014/01/24/politics/zero-tolerance.

Ahern, M.A. (2015, October 8). Former CPS CEO Byrd-Bennett intends to plead guilty in bribery scheme. Nbcchicago.com. Retrieved from: http://www.nbcchicago.com/blogs/ward-room/Former-CPS-CEO-Byrd-Bennett-Could-Be-Charged-in-Contract-Scheme-Report-331306352.html.

Aldeman, C. (2015, February 6). In defense of annual school testing. *New York Times*. Retrieved from: http://www.nytimes.com/2015/02/07/opinion/in-defense-of-annual-school-testing.html.

Almond, L. (Ed.). (2008). *School violence*. Detroit: Greenhaven.

Art Instruction Schools. (2015). Overview. Artinstructionschools.edu. Retrieved from: https://artinstructionschools.edu/The_Program.

Art Students League. (2016). About the art students league of New York. Theartstudentsleague.org. Retrieved from: http://www.theartstudentsleague.org/About.aspx.

Atkeson, S. (2014, October 29). N.Y.C. schools to open doors to student cellphones. *Education Week*. Retrieved from: http://www.edweek.org/ew/articles/2014/10/29/10cellphone.h34.html.

Aubrey, A. (2014, December 10). From potatoes to salty fries in school: Congress tweaks food rules. Npr.org. Retrieved from: http://www.npr.org/blogs/thesalt/2014/12/10/369869222/from-potatoes-to-salty-fries-in-school-congress-tweaks-food-rules.

Badger, E. (2016, October 11). Actually, many "inner cities" are doing great. *New York Times*. Retrieved from: http://www.nytimes.com/2016/10/12/upshot/actually-many-inner-cities-are-doing-great.html.

Banchero, S., & Kesmodel, D. (2011). Teachers are put to the test. Patjehlen.org. Retrieved from: http://www.patjehlen.org/issues/wall-street-journal-reports-testing-companies.

Bartlett, B. (2013, April 2). Dynamic scoring once again. *New York Times*. Retrieved from: http://economix.blogs.nytimes.com/2013/04/02/dynamic-scoring-once-again.

Bellware, K. (2015, October 8). Ex-Chicago schools chief indicted in bribery, kickback scheme. *Huffington Post*. Retrieved from: http://www.huffingtonpost.com/entry/barbara-byrd-bennett-indicted_5616c8fce4b0e66ad4c6fe9e.

Bencin, R. L., & Jonovic, D. J. (1989). *Encyclopedia of telemarketing*. Englewood Cliffs, NJ: Prentice Hall.

Bidwell, A. (2014, August 28). School vouchers: Legal, depending on where you live. *U.S. News & World Report*. Retrieved from: http://www.usnews.com/news/articles/2014/08/28/florida-teachers-parents-sue-state-over-school-voucher-tax-credit.

Bidwell, A. (2015, March 10). Opt-out movement about more than tests, advocates say. *U.S. News*. Retrieved from: http://www.usnews.com/news/articles/2015/03/10/as-students-opt-out-of-common-core-exams-some-say-movement-is-not-about-testing.

Bloomberg unveils redesign of Times Square pedestrian plaza. (2013, December 23). Cbslocal.com. Retrieved from: http://newyork.cbslocal.com/2013/12/23/bloomberg-to-cut-ribbon-on-redesign-of-times-square-pedestrian-plaza.

Blume, H. (2014, April 25). L.A. parents must give OK before iPads sent home with students. *Los Angeles Times*. Retrieved from: http://www.latimes.com/local/lanow/la-me-ln-la-parents-ipads-20140425-story.html.

Bosman, J. (2015, October 8). Ex-Chicago schools head to plead guilty to fraud. *New York Times*. Retrieved from: http://www.nytimes.com/2015/10/09/us/ex-chicago-schools-head-to-plead-guilty-to-fraud.html.

Bouchard, M. (2015, May 16). Graduation is bittersweet as Sweet Briar College is likely closing. *New York Times*. Retrieved from: http://www.nytimes.com/2015/05/17/us/graduation-is-bittersweet-as-sweet-briar-college-is-likely-closing.html.

Brenneman, R. (2015, May 1). Education is political: Can teachers afford not to be? *Education Week*. Retrieved from: http://www.edweek.org/tm/articles/2015/05/01/education-is-political-can-teachers-afford-not.html.

Brody, J. E. (2014, December 22). Why cafeteria food is the best. *New York Times*. Retrieved from: http://well.blogs.nytimes.com/2014/12/22/why-cafeteria-food-is-the-best.

Brody, L. (2015, April 15). More students opt out of N.Y. state exams. *Wall Street Journal*. Retrieved from: http://www.wsj.com/articles/more-students-opt-out-of-n-y-state-exams-1429144870.

Brooks, K. J. (2013, July 17). Projections show fewer A elementaries [*sic*] in Duval, more schools receiving lower grades. *Florida Times-Union*. Retrieved from: http://jacksonville.com/news/schools/2013-07-16/story/projections-show-fewer-elementaries-duval-more-schools-receiving-lower.

Budin, J. (2015, August 21). Everybody hates de Blasio's Times Square overhaul proposal. Curbed.com. Retrieved from: http://ny.curbed.com/archives/2015/08/21/everybody_hates_de_blasios_times_square_overhaul_proposal.php.

Bush, J. (2016). Education reform. Jeb2016.com. Retrieved from: https://jeb2016.com/education/?lang=en.

California Department of Education. (2014, August 18). Parent empowerment. Author. Retrieved from: http://www.cde.ca.gov/ta/ac/pe.

Campos, P. (2014, August 13). The law-school scam. *Atlantic*. Retrieved from: http://www.theatlantic.com/features/archive/2014/08/the-law-school-scam/375069.

Cardwell, D., & Hu, W. (2006, May 15). Cellphones in schools: From irritant to brouhaha. *New York Times*. Retrieved from: http://query.nytimes.com/gst/abstract.html.

Cassidy, C. A. (2015, April 18). At some schools, up to 70 percent of kids are refusing to take the exams. *Time*. Retrieved from: http://time.com/3827395/common-core-opt-out.

Cell phones should not be banned in schools. (2008). Galegroup.com. Retrieved from: http://ic.galegroup.com/ic/ovic/ViewpointsDetailsPage/DocumentToolsPortletWindow?displayGroupName=Viewpoints&jsid=26c55c2126c36f614cd5a17fdcba19ac&action=2&catId=&documentId=GALE%7CEJ3010509225&u=mlin_m_highrock&zid=43a51cc2f9315e7c6f386e31a304693c.

Chen, B. X. (2015, August 31). T-Mobile says it will ban abusers of unlimited data plan. *New York Times*. Retrieved from: http://bits.blogs.nytimes.com/2015/08/31/t-mobile-says-it-will-ban-abusers-of-unlimited-data-plan.

Cheshire, S. (2014, August 19). Healthy school lunches face tough taste test. Cnn.com. Retrieved from: http://www.cnn.com/2014/08/19/health/national-school-lunch-program.

Chicago Public Schools. (2012, October 12). Mayor Emanuel names Barbara Byrd-Bennett new CEO: Lifelong educator becomes leader of CPS. Author. Retrieved from: http://cps.edu/Spotlight/Pages/Spotlight362.aspx.

Chingos, M. (2015, October 26). Breaking the curve: Promises and pitfalls of using NAEP data to assess the state role in student achievement. Urban.org. Retrieved from: http://www.urban.org/research/publication/breaking-curve-promises-and-pitfalls-using-naep-data-assess-state-role-student-achievement.

Choi, C. (2014, October 10). Activist investor Starboard wins control of Darden's board. *Daily Finance*. Retrieved from: http://www.dailyfinance.com/2014/10/10/starboard-wins-control-darden-board.

Choi, C. (2015, September 16). Olive Garden brings back "Pasta Pass." *Cadillac News*. Retrieved from: http://www.cadillacnews.com/ap_story/national_news/20150916_ap_7bc7c0bf02a14b96b00d8fc517dd1940.html.

Chow, A. (2012, April 25). Top 10 law schools that hire their own graduates. Findlaw.com. Retrieved from: http://blogs.findlaw.com/greedy_associates/2012/04/top-10-law-schools-that-hire-their-own-graduates.html.

Clifford, R. A. (2007, Summer). The use of video at trial: A potentially powerful tool. *Trial Journal*. Retrieved from: https://www.iltla.com/publications/the-use-of-video-at-trial-a-potentially-powerful-tool.

Clifford, S. (2015, May 24). A flattering biographical video as the last exhibit for the defense. *New York Times*. Retrieved from: http://www.nytimes.com/2015/05/25/nyregion/defendants-using-biographical-videos-to-show-judges-another-side-at-sentencing.html.

Complaint review: Art instruction schools. (2012, May 11). Ripoffreport.com. Retrieved from: http://www.ripoffreport.com/r/Art-Instruction-Schools/Minneapolis-Minnesota-55413-1745/Art-Instruction-Schools-of-Minneapolis-Minnesota-is-a-ripoff-13768.

Cunningham, J. (2013, October 15). Parent trigger laws in the states. National Conference of State Legislatures. Retrieved from: http://www.ncsl.org/research/education/state-parent-trigger-laws.aspx.

Daniels, P. (Ed.). (2009). *Zero tolerance policies in schools*. Detroit: Greenhaven.

David, J. L. (2010, May). What research says about using value-added measures to evaluate teachers. *ASCD*. Retrieved from: http://www.ascd.org/publications/educational_leadership/may10/vol67/num08/Using_Value-Added_Measures_to_Evaluate_Teachers.aspx.

Dawsey, J., & Gay, M. (2015, August 20). NYC Mayor de Blasio: Times Square pedestrian plaza could be removed. *Wall Street Journal*. Retrieved from: http://www.wsj.com/articles/nyc-mayor-de-blasio-times-square-pedestrian-plaza-could-be-removed-1440100495.

Dayen, D. (2014, September 17). The real Olive Garden scandal: Why greedy hedge funders suddenly care so much about breadsticks. *Salon*. Retrieved from: http://www.salon.com/2014/09/17/the_real_olive_garden_scandal_why_greedy_hedge_funders_suddenly_care_so_much_about_breadsticks.

Decker, G. (2015, May 12). Cuomo throws support behind tax credits for private school scholarships. Ny.chalkbeat.org. Retrieved from: http://ny.chalkbeat.org/2015/05/12/cuomo-throws-support-behind-tax-credits-for-private-school-scholarships/#.VfbyXrmFMos.

Dictionary.com. (2015). Dog whistle. Author. Retrieved from: http://dictionary.reference.com/browse/dog-whistle.

Dillon, S. (2010, August 31). Method to grade teachers provokes battles. *New York Times*. Retrieved from: http://www.nytimes.com/2010/09/01/education/01teacher.html.

Direct Marketing Association. (2015). Give your mailbox a makeover. Dmachoice.org. Retrieved from: https://www.dmachoice.org/register.php.

Dominus, S. (2016, September 7). An effective but exhausting alternative to high-school suspensions. *New York Times*. Retrieved from: http://www.nytimes.com/2016/09/11/magazine/an-effective-ut-exhausting-alternative-to-high-school-suspensions.html.

Donegan, B. (2014, October 20). Controversy erupts over viral photo of paltry-portioned, federally-mandated school lunch. Truthinmedia.com. Retrieved from: http://truthinmedia.com/controversy-erupts-over-viral-photo-of-paltry-portioned-federally-mandated-school-lunch.

Dougherty, J. (2014, May 5). Surveillance video at trial: To use or not to use? Courtroomsciences.com. Retrieved from: http://www.courtroomsciences.com/News/Blog/2014/05/15/Surveillance-Video-at-Trial-To-use-or-not-to-use.

Drum, K. (2014, September 12). Quote of the day: Salt your pasta water, capiche? *Mother Jones*. Retrieved from: http://www.motherjones.com/kevin-drum/2014/09/quote-day-salt-your-pasta-water-capiche.

Efland, A. (1990). *A history of art education: Intellectual and social currents in teaching the visual arts*. New York: Teachers College Press.

Eisner, E. W. (2002). *The arts and the creation of mind*. New Haven, CT: Yale University Press.

Esmonde, D. (2015, April 18). State tests making rebels of parents. *Buffalo News*. Retrieved from: http://www.buffalonews.com/city-region/state-tests-making-rebels-of-parents-20150418.

Evich, H. B. (2014, June 4). Behind the school lunch fight. *Politico*. Retrieved from: http://www.politico.com/story/2014/06/michelle-obama-public-school-lunch-school-nutrition-association-lets-move-107390.
Family's anger over school lunch reveals more widespread issues. (2014, November 5). Okcfox.com. Retrieved from: http://www.okcfox.com/story/26799348/familys-anger-over-school-lunch-reveals-more-widespread-issues.
FBI looked into ex-Chicago schools chief in Detroit. (2015, November 4). *Northwest Herald*. Retrieved from: http://www.nwherald.com/2015/11/04/records-fbi-looked-into-ex-chicago-schools-chief-in-detroit/apdjsup.
Federal school nutrition programs. (2015, June 5). Newamerica.org. Retrieved from: http://atlas.newamerica.org/federal-school-nutrition-programs.
Federal Trade Commission. (2015a). Enforcement. Author. Retrieved from: https://www.ftc.gov/news-events/media-resources/do-not-call-registry/enforcement.
Federal Trade Commission. (2015b). National Do Not Call Registry. Author. Retrieved from: https://www.donotcall.gov.
Feigenson, N., & Spiesel, C. (2009). *Law on display: The digital transformation of legal persuasion and judgment*. New York: New York University Press.
Feldman, C. (2015, January 19). Truancy bill will be hotly debated during the Texas legislative session. *Houston Chronicle*. Retrieved from: http://www.houstonchronicle.com/life/article/Truancy-bill-will-be-hotly-debated-during-the-6012827.php.
Fertig, B. (2013, May 15). Thompson proposes mid-course correction to Bloomberg's school policies. Wnyc.org. Retrieved from: http://www.wnyc.org/story/302288-thompson-proposes-mid-course-correction-to-bloombergs-school-policies.
Fertig, B. (2015, May 20). Who benefits from Cuomo's education tax credit plan. [*sic*] Wnyc.org. Retrieved from: http://www.wnyc.org/story/who-would-win-under-cuomos-education-tax-plan.
Fischer, K. (2014, November 26). New healthy school lunch rules stir controversy as food trash piles up. Healthline.com. Retrieved from: http://www.healthline.com/health-news/new-healthy-school-lunches-stir-controversy-112614.
FitzPatrick, L., & Mihalopoulos, D. (2015, October 26). FBI looked into Byrd-Bennett before she worked in Chicago. *Chicago Sun Times*. Retrieved from: http://chicago.suntimes.com/news/7/71/1041686/hold-hold-fbi-began-investigating-byrd-bennett-worked-chicago.
Fleisher, L. (2012, March 20). Albany boosts private schools. *Wall Street Journal*. Retrieved from: http://www.wsj.com/articles/SB10001424052702304636404577293941502489380.
Flynn, H. (2015, January 7). House passes dynamic scoring. *Politico*. Retrieved from: http://www.politico.com/tipsheets/morning-tax/2015/01/house-passes-dynamic-scoring-ryan-sets-first-ways-and-means-hearing-cbo-director-battle-gets-some-heat-212543.
Forgotten attorney. (2015). Author. Retrieved from: https://forgottenattorney.wordpress.com.
Form tool. (2015). Author. Retrieved from: https://www.theformtool.com/coming-50000-unemployed-lawyers.

Friedman Foundation for Educational Choice. (2016) Florida Tax Credit Scholarship Program. Author. Retrieved from: http://www.edchoice.org/school-choice/programs/florida-tax-credit-scholarship-program.

Fuchs, E. (2013, December 14). I consider law school a waste of my life and an extraordinary waste of money. Businessinsider.com. Retrieved from: http://www.businessinsider.com/is-law-school-worth-the-money-2013-12.

Garrow, H. B. (2013, July 25). Some educators give F to state plan to grade schools. *Virginia Pilot*. Retrieved from: http://www.pilotonline.com/news/government/politics/virginia/some-educators-give-f-to-state-plan-to-grade-schools/article_e34a2548-cbe2-5dbf-8db8-26762eb78a27.html.

Giordano, G. (2000). *Twentieth-century reading education: Understanding practices of today in terms of patterns of the past*. London, UK: Elsevier/JAI Press.

Giordano, G. (2003). *Twentieth-century textbook wars: A history of advocacy and opposition*. New York: Peter Lang.

Giordano, G. (2004). *Wartime schools: How World War II changed American education*. New York: Peter Lang.

Giordano, G. (2005). *How testing came to dominate American schools: The history of educational assessment*. New York: Peter Lang.

Giordano, G. (2007). *American special education: A history of early political advocacy*. New York: Peter Lang.

Giordano, G. (2009). *Solving education problems effectively: A guide to using the case method*. Lanham, MD: Rowman & Littlefield.

Giordano, G. (2010). *Cockeyed education: A case method primer*. Lanham, MD: Rowman & Littlefield.

Giordano, G. (2011). *Lopsided school: Case method briefings*. Lanham, MD: Rowman & Littlefield.

Giordano, G. (2012a). *Capping costs: Putting a price tag on school reform*. Lanham, MD: Rowman & Littlefield.

Giordano, G. (2012b). *Teachers go to rehab: Historical and current advice to instructors*. Lanham, MD: Rowman & Littlefield.

Giordano, G. (2014). *Common sense questions about instruction: The answers can provide essential steps to improvement*. Lanham, MD: Rowman & Littlefield.

Giordano, G. (2015). *Common sense questions about school administration: The answers can provide essential steps to improvement*. Lanham, MD: Rowman & Littlefield.

Giordano, G. (2016). *Common sense questions about testing: The answers can provide essential steps to improvement*. Lanham, MD: Rowman & Littlefield.

Gliksman, S. (2013). *iPad in education for dummies*. New York: Wiley.

Goddard, T. (2015). Dog-whistle politics. *Taegan Goddard's political dictionary*. Retrieved from: politicshttp://politicaldictionary.com/words/dog-whistle-politics.

Goldstein, D. (2015, March 6). Inexcusable absences. Themarshallproject.org. Retrieved from: https://www.themarshallproject.org/2015/03/06/inexcusable-absences.

Goodson, S. (2011, February 16). How to make or break an ad in Times Square. *Forbes*. Retrieved from: http://www.forbes.com/sites/marketshare/2011/02/16/how-to-make-or-break-an-ad-in-times-square.

Gootman, E. (2006a, May 12). Parents leave a message: Let students have their cellphones. *New York Times*. Retrieved from: http://query.nytimes.com/gst/abstract.html?res=9E03E0D8173EF931A25756C0A9609C8B63.

Gootman, E. (2006b, June 15). School phone ban stirs, yes, a lot of talk. *New York Times*. Retrieved from: http://www.nytimes.com/2006/06/15/nyregion/15cellphones.html.

Gormley, J. (2015, May 18). Education tax credit for private schools among Cuomo's priorities this session. *Legislative Gazette*. Retrieved from: http://www.legislativegazette.com/Articles-Top-Stories-c-2015-05-18-91807.113122-Education-tax-credit-for-private-schools-among-Cuomos-priorities-this-session.html.

Government food flight. (2015, October 15). *Wall Street Journal*. Retrieved from: http://www.wsj.com/articles/government-food-flight-1444949683.

Grannan, C. (2012, March 20). Triggers create nothing but chaos and division. *New York Times*. Retrieved from: http://www.nytimes.com/roomfordebate/2012/03/18/hopes-and-feard-for-parent-trigger-laws/triggers-create-nothing-but-chaos-and-division.

Green, P. (2015, April 23). The independent women of Sweet Briar. *New York Times*. Retrieved from: http://www.nytimes.com/2015/04/23/fashion/the-independent-women-of-sweet-briar.html.

Grynbaum, M. M., & Flegenheimer, M. (2015, August 20). Mayor de Blasio raises prospect of removing Times Square pedestrian plazas. *New York Times*. Retrieved from: http://www.nytimes.com/2015/08/21/nyregion/mayor-de-blasio-raises-prospect-of-removing-times-square-pedestrian-plazas.html.

Harper, S. J. (2015, August 25). Too many law students, too few legal jobs. *New York Times*. Retrieved from: http://www.nytimes.com/2015/08/25/opinion/too-many-law-students-too-few-legal-jobs.html.

Harris, E. A. (2015a, October 26). Merryl Tisch, Board of Regents Chancellor, is stepping down. *New York Times*. Retrieved from: http://www.nytimes.com/2015/10/27/nyregion/merryl-tisch-board-of-regents-chancellor-says-she-will-step-down.html.

Harris, E. A. (2015b, April 23). Only alternative for some students sitting out standardized tests: Do nothing. *New York Times*. Retrieved from: http://www.nytimes.com/2015/04/24/nyregion/only-alternative-for-some-students-sitting-out-standardized-tests-do-nothing.html.

Harris, E. A., & Fessenden, F. (2015, May 20). "Opt out" becomes anti-test rallying cry in New York state. *New York Times*. Retrieved from: http://www.nytimes.com/2015/05/21/nyregion/opt-out-movement-against-common-core-testing-grows-in-new-york-state.html.

Heller, S. (2008, December 3). Draw me schools of commercial art. Designobserver.com. Retrieved from: http://designobserver.com/feature/draw-me-schools-of-commercial-art/7687.

Hennick, C. (2013, November 3). High-tech gear in schools offers lesson in economics. *Boston Globe*. Retrieved from: https://www.bostonglobe.com/metro/regionals/west/2013/11/03/become-ipads-devices-great-rigeur-schools-offers-lesson-should-economics-ipads-students-high-tech-gear-schools-call-tablets-high-tech/2AvVcGYtZIlq9YKyTO8TEK/story.html.

Hernández, J. C. (2013, June 21). Grading problems with regents [*sic*] exams delay some diplomas. *New York Times*. Retrieved from: http://www.nytimes.com/2013/06/22/nyregion/grading-problems-with-regents-exams-delay-some-diplomas.html.

Hope, L. (2015, June 1). Barbara Byrd-Bennett resigns from CPS. Abc7chicago.com. Retrieved from: http://abc7chicago.com/education/barbara-byrd-bennett-resigns-from-cps/759838.

Hope, M. (2014, July 8). Michelle Obama's federal forced food efforts stir controversy. Breitbart.com. Retrieved from: http://www.breitbart.com/texas/2014/07/08/michelle-obama-s-federal-forced-food-efforts-stir-controversy.

Illinois: Ex-Chicago schools chief pleads guilty in contract scheme. (2015, October 13). *New York Times*. Retrieved from: http://www.nytimes.com/2015/10/14/us/illinois-ex-chicago-schools-chief-pleads-guilty-in-contract-scheme.html.

Ip, G. (2015, March 25). Dynamic scoring: A potential super model. *Wall Street Journal*. Retrieved from: http://www.wsj.com/articles/dynamic-scoring-a-potential-super-model-1427307531.

iPad management: Tips for educators. (2013). Educationworld.com. Retrieved from: http://www.educationworld.com/a_tech/educator-ipad-management-tips.shtml.

Jacobs, C. (2015, June 11). CBO dynamic scoring: how Obamacare's "poverty trap" impedes economic growth. *Wall Street Journal*. Retrieved from: http://blogs.wsj.com/washwire/2015/06/11/cbo-dynamic-scoring-how-obamacares-poverty-trap-impedes-economic-growth.

Jacobs, P. (2014, October 16). Here's why a controversial plan to give an iPad to every Los Angeles public school student failed. Businessinsider.com. Retrieved from: http://www.businessinsider.com/why-controversial-plan-to-give-ipads-to-la-public-school-students-failed-2014–10.

Jeb Bush on education. (2015, December 7). Ontheissues.org. Retrieved from: http://www.ontheissues.org/2016/Jeb_Bush_Education.htm.

Kaplan, T. (2015, May 17). Cuomo promotes tax credits for families of students at private schools. *New York Times*. Retrieved from: http://www.nytimes.com/2015/05/18/nyregion/cuomo-promotes-tax-credits-for-families-of-students-at-private-schools.html.

Keating, L. (2015, September 2). T-Mobile plans to ban abusers of its unlimited data plan. Techtimes.com. Retrieved from: http://www.techtimes.com/articles/81392/20150902/t-mobile-plans-ban-abusers-unlimited-data-plan.htm.

Kessenides, D. (2014, June 20). Jobs are still scarce for new law school grads. *Bloomberg Business*. Retrieved from: http://www.bloomberg.com/bw/articles/2014-06-20/the-employment-rate-falls-again-for-recent-law-school-graduates.

Key, P. (2016, August 19). Dean: Trump has been "dog whistling for an entire year." Breitbart.com. Retrieved from: http://www.breitbart.com/video/2016/08/19/dean-trump-has-been-dog-whistling-for-an-entire-year.

Kiema, K. (2015, February 23). As schools lift bans on cell phones, educators weigh pros and cons. *NEA Today*. Retrieved from: http://neatoday.org/2015/02/23/school-cell-phone-bans-end-educators-weigh-pros-cons.

Kimmelman, M. (2015, August 21). Challenging Mayor de Blasio over Times Square plazas. *New York Times*. Retrieved from: http://www.nytimes.com/2015/08/22/arts/design/challenging-mayor-de-blasio-over-times-square-plazas.html.

Krugman, P. (2014, March 16). That old-time whistle. *New York Times*. Retrieved from: http://www.nytimes.com/2014/03/17/opinion/krugman-that-old-time-whistle.html.

Krugman, P. (2015, January 13). Selective voodoo. *New York Times*. Retrieved from: http://krugman.blogs.nytimes.com/2015/01/13/selective-voodoo.

LA Rev Stat § 17:233. (2015). Justia.com. Retrieved from: http://law.justia.com/codes/louisiana/2011/rs/title17/rs17-233.

LaRaviere, T. (2015, October 17). Cut, contradict, and collect: Byrd-Bennett & the Emanuel way. Troylaraviere.net. Retrieved from: http://troylaraviere.net/2015/10/17/cut-contradict-and-collect-byrd-bennett-the-emanuel-way.

Leonhardt, D. (2015, October 26). Surprise: Florida and Texas excel in math and reading scores. *New York Times*. Retrieved from: http://www.nytimes.com/2015/10/27/upshot/surprise-florida-and-texas-excel-in-math-and-reading-scores.html.

Lerum, E. (2012, November 29). De-bunking some common myths about parent trigger. *Huffington Post*. Retrieved from: http://www.huffingtonpost.com/eric-lerum/parent-trigger-laws_b_1924453.html.

Lieberman, J. (2008). *School shootings: What every parent and educator needs to know to protect our children*. New York: Citadel.

Lindsay, S. (2015, October 20). Is grade inflation in high school real? Prepscholar.com. Retrieved from: http://blog.prepscholar.com/grade-inflation-high-school.

Lindstrom, N. (2014, May 27). At a south LA school, change without a battle over "parent trigger" law. *Huffington Post*. Retrieved from: http://www.huffingtonpost.com/2014/05/27/west-athens-parent-trigger_n_5398008.html.

Linnell-Olsen, L. (2015). Everything you want to know about school lunch controversy. Parentinginschools.about.com. Retrieved from: http://parentinginschools.about.com/od/School-Lunch-And-Nutrition/fl/Everything-You-Want-to-Know-About-School-Lunch-Controversy.htm.

Litigation Technology Services. (2011). Frequently asked questions about deposition videography. Author. Retrieved from: http://www.digitalcasemanagement.com/Frequently.html.

Lochhead, C. (2014, August 15). School lunch standards feed $10 billion controversy in D.C. Sfgate.com. Retrieved from: http://www.sfgate.com/health/article/School-lunch-standards-feed-10-billion-5529696.php.

Lysiak, M. (2013). *Newtown: An American tragedy*. New York: Gallery.

Madhani, A. (2015, October 13). Ex-Chicago schools chief pleads guilty to steering $23 million in contracts. *USA TODAY*. Retrieved from: http://www.usatoday.com/story/news/2015/10/13/chicago-public-schools-barbard-byrd-bennett-expected-to-plead-guilty/73858752.

Mangu-Ward, K. (2013, March 1). Pop-tart pistol: 7-year-old gets suspended for gun-shaped pastry. Reason.com. Retrieved from: http://reason.com/blog/2013/03/01/pop-tart-pistol-7-year-old-gets-suspende.

Marcos, C. (2015, January 6). House adopts "dynamic scoring" rule. Thehill. com. Retrieved from: http://thehill.com/blogs/floor-action/house/228684-house-adopts-dynamic-scoring-rule.

Martinez, B. (2010, October 18). Blending computers into classrooms. *Wall Street Journal*. Retrieved from: http://www.wsj.com/articles/SB10001424052702304772804575558383085638118.

Maxwell, L. A. (2009, October 28). L.A. gives parents "trigger" to restructure schools: New rules will give parents of children in struggling schools the power to make changes. *Education Week*. Retrieved from: http://www.edweek.org/ew/articles/2009/10/28/10lausd.h29.html?tkn=XSPFlsFbBWuvkwgrU5648hQoUCY%2FsLhxVSqK.

May, D. C. (2014). *School safety in the United States: A reasoned look at the rhetoric.* Durham, NC: Carolina Academic Press.

McCutcheon, C. (2014). *Dog whistles, walk-backs, and Washington handshakes: Decoding the jargon, slang, and. . .[sic].* Lebanon, NH: ForEdge.

McGeehan, P., & Grynbaum, M. M. (2015, September 30). Limits put forth for topless performers in Times Square. *New York Times*. Retrieved from: http://www.nytimes.com/2015/10/01/nyregion/limits-put-forth-for-topless-performers-in-times-square.html.

McGray, D. (2009, May 11). The instigator: A crusader's plan to remake failing schools. *New Yorker*. Retrieved from: http://www.newyorker.com/magazine/2009/05/11/the-instigator.

McHatton, R. J. (1988). *Total telemarketing*. New York: Wiley.

McKenna, L. (2015, March 10). The unfortunate fate of Sweet Briar's professors. *Atlantic*. Retrieved from: http://www.theatlantic.com/education/archive/2015/03/the-unfortunate-fate-of-sweet-briars-professors/387376.

McWilliams, I. A. (2009, July 1). Lights, camera, action: Getting the most out of videos at trial. Thejuryexpert.com. Retrieved from: http://www.thejuryexpert.com/2009/07/lights-camera-action-getting-the-most-out-of-videos-at-trial.

Meier, P. (2002, August 18). DRAW ME. *Star Tribune*. Retrieved from: https://www.highbeam.com/doc/1G1-90510386.html.

Meisner, J., & Perez, J. (2015, October 8). Former Chicago Public Schools chief to plead guilty to bribery scheme. *Chicago Tribune*. Retrieved from: http://www.chicagotribune.com/news/local/breaking/ct-barbara-byrd-bennett-chicago-public-schools-charged-met-20151008-story.html.

Mencimer, S. (2011, November/December). Jeb Bush's cyber attack on public schools. *Mother Jones*. Retrieved from: http://www.motherjones.com/politics/2011/10/jeb-bush-digitial-learning-public-schools.

Mikoulianitch, A. (2012, June 18). Doomsday for law school graduates: More bad news. *Business Insider*. Retrieved from: http://www.businessinsider.com/shocking-law-grad-unemployment-way-worse-than-we-thought-book-slamming-law-schools-confirms-it-2012-6.

Miller, S. M., & McVee, M. B. (Eds.). (2012). *Multimodal composing in classrooms: Learning and teaching for the digital world.* New York: Routledge.

Milne-Tyte, A. (2014, March 28). Comparing law school rankings—Read the fine print. Npr.org. Retrieved from: http://www.npr.org/blogs/money/2014/03/28/294887683/comparing-law-school-rankings-read-the-fine-print.

Moser, L. (2015, October 9). Ex-Chicago schools chief indicted in bribery scheme. *Slate*. Retrieved from: http://www.slate.com/blogs/schooled/2015/10/09/barbara_byrd_bennett_corruption_indictment_ex_cps_ceo_cooperates_with_investigation.html.

Murphy, M. E. (2014, August 5). Why some schools are selling all their iPads. *The Atlantic*. Retrieved from: http://www.theatlantic.com/education/archive/2014/08/whats-the-best-device-for-interactive-learning/375567.

National Center for Fair and Open Testing. (2015). Just say no to the test. Author. Retrieved from: http://www.fairtest.org/get-involved/opting-out.

Neff, B. (2015, August 19). Christie: Improve schools by giving every kid their own iPad. *Daily Caller*. Retrieved from: http://dailycaller.com/2015/08/19/christie-improve-schools-by-giving-every-kid-their-own-ipad.

Nelson, E. (2014, June 12). House delays vote on school lunch controversy. *USA TODAY*. Retrieved from: http://www.usatoday.com/story/news/politics/2014/06/12/school-lunch-nutrition-vote/10394667.

New York City Charter School Center. (2015). Author. Retrieved from: http://www.nyccharterschools.org.

New York State United Teachers. (2015a, April 2). NYSUT Q&A on opting out. Nysut.org. Retrieved from: http://www.nysut.org/news/2015/april/nysut-q-and-a-on-opting-out.

New York State United Teachers. (2015b, May 18). NYSUT ad takes aim at tax credit. Author. Retrieved from: http://www.nysut.org/news/2015/may/audio-nysut-ad-takes-aim-at-tax-credit.

New York Times Editorial Board. (2009, December 31). Mr. Bloomberg's third term. *New York Times*. Retrieved from: http://www.nytimes.com/2010/01/01/opinion/01fri1.html.

New York Times Editorial Board. (2014, December 6). Keeping score on the budget. *New York Times*. Retrieved from: http://www.nytimes.com/2014/12/07/opinion/sunday/keeping-score-on-the-budget.html.

New York Times Editorial Board. (2015a, October 24). The law school debt crisis. *New York Times*. Retrieved from: http://www.nytimes.com/2015/10/25/opinion/sunday/the-law-school-debt-crisis.html.

New York Times Editorial Board. (2015b, October 30). Why the Republican tax plans won't work. *New York Times*. Retrieved from: http://www.nytimes.com/2015/10/31/opinion/why-the-republican-tax-plans-wont-work.html.

Newsday Editorial Board. (2015, April 18). The opt-out inferno: How did Long Island get here? *Newsday*. Retrieved from: http://www.newsday.com/opinion/the-opt-out-inferno-how-did-long-island-get-here-1.10289277.

Nichols, J. A. (2013). *iPads in the library: Using tablet technology to enhance programs for all ages*. Santa Barbara, CA: Libraries Unlimited.

NYS ALLIES for Public Education. (2015, April). Refusal letter. Author. Retrieved from: http://www.nysape.org/refusal-letter.html#sthash.JnKqms5z.dpuf.

Parent-trigger war escalates. (2012, August 28). *Wall Street Journal*. Retrieved from: http://www.wsj.com/articles/SB10000872396390444270404577607432751373136.

Parks, P. J. (2009). *School violence*. San Diego, CA: ReferencePoint.

Perez, J. (2015, October 9). Emanuel supports principal training amid CPS scandal fallout. *Chicago Tribune*. Retrieved from: http://www.chicagotribune.com/news/ct-chicago-school-principal-training-future-met-20151009-story.html.

Pillow, T. (2014, February 6). Pop-Tart school-gun bill clears first hurdle in Florida. *USA TODAY*. Retrieved from: http://www.usatoday.com/story/news/politics/2014/02/07/pop-tart-gun-bill/5254629.

Pogue, D. (2011, February 24). A parent's struggle with a child's iPad addiction. *New York Times*. Retrieved from: http://pogue.blogs.nytimes.com/2011/02/24/a-parents-struggle-with-a-childs-ipad-addiction.

Popovich, N. (2014, June 23). Do US laws that punish parents for truancy keep their kids in school? *The Guardian*. Retrieved from: http://www.theguardian.com/education/2014/jun/23/-sp-school-truancy-fines-jail-parents-punishment-children.

Quirk, M. B. (2015, September 17). Olive Garden Pasta Passes sell out in under a second: Were you able to score one? Consumerist.com. Retrieved from: http://consumerist.com/2015/09/17/olive-garden-pasta-passes-sell-out-in-under-a-second-were-you-able-to-score-one.

Raudenbush, S. W., & Jean, M. (2012, October 15). How should educators interpret value-added scores? Carnegieknowledgenetwork.org. Retrieved from: http://www.carnegieknowledgenetwork.org/briefs/value-added/interpreting-value-added.

Reynolds, G. H. (2013, March 11). Public school insanity. *USA TODAY*. Retrieved from: http://www.usatoday.com/story/opinion/2013/03/11/schools-guns-suspensions-education-column/1976751.

Ribble, M. (2011). *Digital citizenship in schools*. Eugene, OR: International Society for Technology in Education.

Rich, M. (2014, July 8). Departure of official is sought by teachers. *New York Times*. Retrieved from: http://www.nytimes.com/2014/07/09/us/departure-of-official-is-sought-by-teachers.html.

Rich, M. (2015, November 19). Negotiators come to agreement on revising No Child Left Behind Law. *New York Times*. Retrieved from: http://www.nytimes.com/2015/11/20/us/negotiators-come-to-agreement-on-revising-no-child-left-behind-law.html.

Rimel, A. (2014, January 10). Parents organize opposition to Corvallis schools iPads. *Corvallis Gazette-Times*. Retrieved from: http://www.gazettetimes.com/news/local/education/parents-organize-opposition-to-corvallis-schools-ipads/article_615bf2da-799e-11e3-ab77-001a4bcf887a.html.

Rizga, K. (2011, April 7). The battle over charter schools. *Mother Jones*. Retrieved from: http://www.motherjones.com/politics/2011/03/parent-trigger-compton-NCLB.

Rowell, K., & McGlothlin, J. (2015, September 21). Parents, not schools, should decide what to pack for lunch. *New York Times*. Retrieved from: http://parenting.blogs.nytimes.com/2015/09/21/parents-not-schools-should-decide-what-to-pack-for-lunch.

Sanchez, C. (2015, November 24). Goodbye, No Child Left Behind. Npr.org. Retrieved from: http://www.npr.org/sections/ed/2015/11/24/456795140/goodbye-no-child-left-behind.

Schick, A. (2015, June 11). The brawl over tax credits for religious schools. *Wall Street Journal*. Retrieved from: http://www.wsj.com/articles/the-brawl-over-tax-credits-for-religious-schools-1434064276.

Schug, M. C., & Niederjohn, M. S. (2009). Value added testing: Improving state testing and teacher compensation in Wisconsin. Wpri.org. Retrieved from: http://www.wpri.org/WPRI/Reports/2009/Value-Added-Testing-Improving-State-Testing-and-Teacher-Compensation-in-Wisconsin.htm.

Schulten, K. (2013, December 12). Does your school hand out too many A's? *New York Times*. Retrieved from: http://learning.blogs.nytimes.com/2013/12/12/does-your-school-hand-out-too-many-as.

Schutz, P. (2015, October 12). More Barbara Byrd-Bennett CPS contracts under scrutiny. Wttw.com. Retrieved from: http://chicagotonight.wttw.com/2015/10/12/more-barbara-byrd-bennett-cps-contracts-under-scrutiny.

Schwartz, L. G. (2009). *Mechanical witness: A history of motion picture evidence in U.S. courts*. Oxford, UK: Oxford University Press.

Shapiro, E. (2015, January 7). De Blasio, Fariña leave cell phone discipline to schools. Capitalnewyork.com. Retrieved from: http://www.capitalnewyork.com/article/city-hall/2015/01/8559736/de-blasio-fari%C3%B1a-leave-cell-phone-discipline-schools.

Should we allow students to use their cell phones in school? (2011, February). *Educational Leadership*. Retrieved from: http://www.ascd.org/publications/educational-leadership/feb11/vol68/num05/Should-We-Allow-Students-to-Use-Their-Cell-Phones-in-School%C2%A2.aspx.

Silets, A. (2015, October 12). Examining the indictment of Barbara Byrd-Bennett. Wttw.com. Retrieved from: http://chicagotonight.wttw.com/2015/10/12/examining-indictment-barbara-byrd-bennett.

Stokols, E. (2015, March 15). Jeb: Trump using racial "dog whistle." *Politico*. Retrieved from: http://www.politico.com/story/2015/09/bush-trump-dog-whistle-213334.

Stolberg, S. G. (2015a, March 22). Anger and activism greet plan to shut Sweet Briar College. *New York Times*. Retrieved from: http://www.nytimes.com/2015/03/23/education/sweet-briars-imminent-closing-stirs-small-uprising-in-a-college-idyll.html.

Stolberg, S. G. (2015b, March 30). Virginia: Suit seeks to prevent college from closing. *New York Times*. Retrieved from: http://www.nytimes.com/2015/03/31/us/virginia-suit-seeks-to-prevent-sweet-briar-college-from-closing.html.

Stolberg, S. G. (2015c, June 23). Sweet Briar College is saved but is not in the clear. *New York Times*. Retrieved from: http://www.nytimes.com/2015/06/24/us/sweet-briar-collegeis-saved-but-not-in-the-clear.html.

Stolle, M. (2015, June 19). Report reveals students', parents' feelings about iPad program. *Post Bulletin*. Retrieved from: http://www.postbulletin.com/news/local/report-reveals-students-parents-feelings-about-ipad-program/article_6d73c704-72ab-570d-80e4-368da56903a7.html.

Stone, B., & Wyman, J. (1992). *Successful telemarketing*. Lincolnwood, IL: NTC Business Books.
Stopping network abusers: FAQs (2015, October 5). T-mobile.com. Retrieved from: https://support.t-mobile.com/docs/DOC-23577.
SUPES Academy (2015). There is a crisis of leadership. Author. Retrieved from: https://k12leaders.squarespace.com.
Tata, S., & Ford, J. (2014, April 1). Family opts out of "bullying" Common Core exams. Pix11.com. Retrieved from: http://pix11.com/2014/04/01/family-opts-out-of-bullying-common-core-exams.
Taylor, K., & Rich, M. (2015, April 20). Teachers' unions fight standardized testing, and find diverse allies. *New York Times*. Retrieved from: http://www.nytimes.com/2015/04/21/education/teachers-unions-reasserting-themselves-with-push-against-standardized-testing.html.
Texas decriminalizing students' truancy. (2015, June 20). *USA TODAY*. Retrieved from: http://www.usatoday.com/story/news/nation/2015/06/20/texas-truancy-absent-students-criminalized/29047285.
Texas honor student jailed for missing too much school. (2012, May 25). Cbs46.com. Retrieved from: http://www.cbs46.com/story/18626605/texas-honors-student-jailed-for-excessive-truancy.
Texas law decriminalizes school truancy. (2015, June 20). *New York Times*. Retrieved from: http://www.nytimes.com/2015/06/21/us/texas-law-decriminalizes-school-truancy.html.
Thompson, A. (2014, November 21). Crackdown on truancy focuses on parents. Wreg.com. Retrieved from: http://wreg.com/2014/11/21/crackdown-on-truancy-focuses-on-parents.
Times Square transformation. (2015). Timessquarenyc.org. Retrieved from: http://www.timessquarenyc.org/live-work/times-square-transformation/index.aspx#.VgwRIbmFPQk.
Treaster, J. B. (2015, July 31). Liberal arts, a lost cause? *New York Times*. Retrieved from: http://www.nytimes.com/2015/08/02/education/edlife/liberal-arts-a-lost-cause.html.
Turner, J. (2016, July 22). New grading system gives schools meaningless bonus points. *Florida Times-Union*. Retrieved from: http://jacksonville.com/opinion/letters-readers/2016-07-22/story/sundays-letters-new-grading-system-gives-schools.
Tyre, P. (2011, September 18). Putting parents in charge. *New York Times*. Retrieved from: http://www.nytimes.com/2011/09/18/opinion/sunday/new-school-trigger-laws-take-parent-engagement-to-a-new-level.html.
Ujifusa, A. (2015, November 25). Teacher, school accountability systems shaken up. *Education Week*. Retrieved from: http://www.edweek.org/ew/articles/2014/06/11/35accountability.h33.html.
Unemployed lawyer. (2011). Author. Retrieved from: https://unemployedlawyer.wordpress.com.
U.S. Department of Agriculture. (2014, March 3). School meals. Author. Retrieved from: http://www.fns.usda.gov/school-meals/healthy-hunger-free-kids-act.
U.S. Government. (2015, February 2). Telemarketing and junk mail. Author. Retrieved from: http://www.usa.gov/topics/family/privacy-protection/junk-mail.shtml.

Vara, V. (2014, September 15). What's the deal with Olive Garden? *New Yorker*. Retrieved from: http://www.newyorker.com/business/currency/whats-deal-olive-garden.

Vitello, P. (2006, June 12). A ring tone meant to fall on deaf ears. *New York Times*. Retrieved from: http://www.nytimes.com/2006/06/12/technology/12ring.html.

Wall Street Journal Editorial Board. (2015, October 30). Obama's education report card. *Wall Street Journal*. Retrieved from: http://www.wsj.com/articles/obamas-education-report-card-1446074804.

Wallace, K. (2015, April 17). Parents all over U.S. "opting out" of standardized student testing. Cnn.com. Retrieved from: http://www.cnn.com/2015/04/17/living/parents-movement-opt-out-of-testing-feat.

Walters, N. (2015, March 24). Some Kanawha County, WV parents don't want county iPads sent home. Wowktv.com. Retrieved from: http://www.wowktv.com/story/28605720/some-kanawha-county-wv-parents-dont-want-county-ipads-sent-home.

Washington Post Editorial Board. (2015, January 12). The risks of the new dynamic scoring rule. *Washington Post*. Retrieved from: http://www.washingtonpost.com/opinions/the-risks-of-the-new-dynamic-scoring-rule/2015/01/12/17d46eaa-983b-11e4-aabd-d0b93ff613d5_story.html.

Weaver, T. (2015, May 20). How far would Cuomo's private school tuition tax break go in Onondaga County? *Post-Standard*. Retrieved from: http://www.syracuse.com/schools/index.ssf/2015/05/how_far_would_cuomos_private_school_tuition_tax_break_go_in_onondaga_county.html.

Webster, N. C. (2015, August 8). Highland parents navigate iPad world with kids. *Chicago Tribune*. Retrieved from: http://www.chicagotribune.com/suburbs/post-tribune/news/ct-ptb-highland-ipad-training-st-0810-20150808-story.html.

Weissmann, J. (2014, September 12). Olive Garden has been committing a culinary crime against humanity. *Slate*. Retrieved from: http://www.slate.com/blogs/moneybox/2014/09/12/olive_garden_doesn_t_salt_its_pasta_water_investors_reveal_a_culinary_crime.html.

Welch, C. (2015, August 31). T-Mobile will now punish customers who abuse unlimited data. Theverge.com. Retrieved from: http://www.theverge.com/2015/8/31/9230595/t-mobile-unlimited-data-tethering-warning.

Wet Canvas. (2016). Wet canvas forums. Wetcanvas.com. Retrieved from: http://www.wetcanvas.com/forums/showthread.php?t=152266.

Whitford, E. (2015, August 20). De Blasio: Erasing Times Square pedestrian plazas might solve our topless painted lady "problem." Gothamist.com. Retrieved from: http://gothamist.com/2015/08/20/deblasio_pedestrian_plazas.php#photo-1.

Wilkie, C. (2015, August 26). Texas sends thousands of kids to court and fines them for missing school: That's about to change. *Huffington Post*. Retrieved from: http://www.huffingtonpost.com/entry/texas-schools-truancy-school-prison_55db67a1e4b08cd3359cd4eb.

Willis, L. (2013). *Electronic devices in schools*. Detroit: Greenhaven.

Wolff, T. F., & Geahigan, G. (1997). *Art criticism and education*. Urbana: University of Illinois Press.

Wood, D. B. (2010, January 7). California's education reforms hand more power to parents. *Christian Science Monitor*. Retrieved from: http://www.csmonitor.com/USA/Education/2010/0107/California-s-education-reforms-hand-more-power-to-parents.

Yarbrough, B. (2013, July 14). LAUSD parent trigger law targets Weigand Elementary School's administrators. *Huffington Post*. Retrieved from: http://www.huffingtonpost.com/2013/05/14/lausd-parent-trigger-_n_3270039.html.

Zaretsky, S. (2015, February 19). An unemployed lawyer's words of wisdom: Not all of us are "financially stable." Abovethelaw.com. Retrieved from: http://abovethelaw.com/2015/02/an-unemployed-lawyers-words-of-wisdom-not-all-of-us-are-financially-stable.

Zimmer, B. (2014, May 23). "Dog whistles" only some voters hear. *Wall Street Journal*. Retrieved from: http://www.wsj.com/articles/SB10001424052702304479704579577953445124862.

Zimmer, B. (2015, April 24). More parents opt in to "opt out." *Wall Street Journal*. Retrieved from: http://www.wsj.com/articles/more-parents-opt-into-opt-out-1429893574.

Zorn, B. (2015, June 15). Common Core is leaving my students behind. *Wall Street Journal*. Retrieved from: http://www.wsj.com/articles/common-core-is-leaving-my-students-behind-1434410461.

About the Author

Gerard Giordano is professor at the University of North Florida. He has written more than a dozen books, including *Common Sense Questions about Instruction*, *Common Sense Questions about School Administration*, and *Common Sense Questions about Tests*. These and other recent books were published by Rowman & Littlefield.

www.ingramcontent.com/pod-product-compliance
Lightning Source LLC
Chambersburg PA
CBHW021852300426
44115CB00005B/123